The Welsh Poems

Also by Peter Finch

Poetry

Wanted For Writing Poetry (with Steve Morris) — *Second Aeon*, 1968
Pieces Of The Universe — *Second Aeon*, 1969
Cycle Of the Suns — *Art Living*,1970
Beyond The Silence — *Vertigo*, 1970
An Alteration In The Way I Breathe — *Quickest way Out*, 1970
The Edge Of Tomorrow (with Jeanne Rushton) — *BB Books*, 1971
The End Of The Vision — *John Jones Ltd*, 1971
Whitesung — *Aquila*, 1972
Antarktika — *Writers Forum*, 1972
Blats — *Second Aeon*, 1973
Trowch Eich Radio 'Mlaen — *Writers Forum*, 1977
Connecting Tubes — *Writers Forum*, 1980
Big Band Dance Music — *Balsam Flex*, 1980
Visual Texts 1970—1980 — (microfiche edition) *Pyrofiche*, 1981
The O Poems — *Writers Forum*, 1981
Blues And Heartbreakers — *Galloping Dog*, 1981
Dances Interdites — *Balsam Flex*, 1982
Some Music And A Little War — *Rivelin Grapheme*, 1984
On Criticism — *Writers Forum*, 1984
Reds In The Bed — *Galloping Dog*, 1985
The Italian Job (with Bob Cobbing) — *Klinker Soundz*, 1985
Selected Poems — *Poetry Wales Press*, 1987
Make — *Galloping Dog*, 1990
Cheng Man Ching Variations — *Writers Forum*, 1990
Poems For Ghosts — *Seren Books*, 1991
Five Hundred Cobbings — *Writers Forum*, 1994
The Spe ell — *Writers Forum*, 1995
Useful — *Seren Books*,1997
Dauber — *Writers Forum*, 1997
Antibodies — *Stride*, 1997
Food — *Seren Books*, 2001
Vizet — Water — *Konkret Konyvek*, 2003
New & Selected Later Poems – *Seren Books*, 2007

As Editor

Typewriter Poems — *Something Else Press*, 1972
Green Horse (with Meic Stephens) — *Christopher Davies*, 1978
The Big Book of Cardiff (with Grahame Davies) – *Seren Books* 2005

Peter Finch

The Welsh Poems

Shearsman Books
2006

Published in the United Kingdom in 2006 by
Shearsman Books Ltd
58 Velwell Road
Exeter EX4 4LD

ISBN-10 0-907562-91-4

ISBN-13 978-0-907562-91-7

Acknowledgements

Some of these poems, often in earlier incarnations, have previously appeared in the following magazines: *And, New Welsh Review, Open Wide Magazine, Sampler, Scratch, Skald, Symtex & Grimmer,* and *The Wading Through Deep Water.* 'Cover Blown' and 'Once You Know Where To Point' appeared in the Stride anthology *My Kind Of Angel: In Memoriam William Burroughs. Cardiff Medicine* in a reworked form appears in *Real Cardiff Two (Seren 2004). Past Interests* is derived from an interview which appeared in *Binary Myths* by Andy Brown *(Stride2003).* Some pieces appeared in the web journals *Muse Apprentice Guild, The Argotist* and *Stride Magazine On Line* as well as in *The Peter Finch Archive.*

The complete *R S Thomas Information* forms a major section of *The Peter Finch Archive* which can be found at peterfinch.co.uk. The text also adorns the BT Internet Data Centre building in Cardiff Bay. *Ysbwriel* in its final form runs along the top of the Lamby Way Landfill site in south east Cardiff and is visible across the river from the Pengam Green Tesco supermarket car park.

The publisher gratefully acknowledges financial assistance from Arts Council England.

Contents

R S Thomas Information

for Sue

Fold

We (us) (I) (you) were (weren't) (won't) (will) a (the) (this)
people (pointed sticks) (prime numbers) (purple patch) taut
(tired) (tiled) (tight as fists) for (from) (frightened) (foaming)
war (wet fish) (wet fist) (wet fear); the (those) (these)
hills (hovering) (hollow) (high) (high) (high) (heated)
(hardened) were (will not) (can not) (can) no
(none) (neither) (normal) harder (holding) (heaving)
(happy as barber's poles) (hard hosts) (home)

I (we) won't (will) the (those) (that) pointed
(printed) (prattle) stick (stack) (steaming) (coal) (coal)
tired (tilted) (hilltop) (hold) from (fear) (fear) (fear)
(fear) (fear) (refute) wet (wash-off) (westerly) (unwound)
those (this) (these) hovering (unheated) (unworn)
(unbilleted) (unbound) will not (can't) none
(no more) holding (fingertip) (finger-stall)
(finger-push) (thrust) look up (look up)
unshaped (unsure) (uncertain) (unable) like us
(fold) (fold) (fold) folded (fold).

Colon

Cilmeri • Battle of Tryweryn • Battle of Maes Madog • Battle of Brecon • Battle of Mynydd Carn • Battle of Lougher • Battle of Lewes • Battle of Evesham • Battle of Haverfordwest • Battle of Laugharne • Battle of Grosmont • Battle of Blackwood Woods • Battle of Casnewydd • Battle of the River Usk • Battle of Pwllmelyn • Battle of Môn • Battle of Port Dinorwic • Battle of Deganwy • Battle of Harlech • Battle of Castell Bere • Battle of Bala • Battle of Cefn Carnedd • Battle of Irfon Bridge • Battle of Welshpool • Battle of Long Mountain • Battle of Gwen Ystrad • Battle of Llanishen Reservoir • Battle of the Cells of Berwyn • Battle of Campstone Hill • Battle of St Fagans • Battle of Catterick • Battle of Camlann • Battle of Arfderydd • Battle of Halifax St Johns Square • Battle of the Bleeding Lance • Battle of Stalling Down • Battle of Clywedog • Battle of Brynmawr Rubber Factory • Battle of Sycharth • Battle of Glyndyfrdwy • Battle of Woodbury Hill • Battle of Swain's Sea • Battle of Mortimer's Cross • Battle of Archensfield • Battle of Cadnant • Battle of Puffin Island • Battle of Llangorse Lake • Battle of the Sacred Groves • The Battle of Bangor Is-Coed • Battle of Rhuddlan • Battle of Castell Caerdydd • Battle of Pembroke • Battle of Orewyn Bridge • Battle of Pwll Melyn • Battle of Cardigan Island • Battle of the fish henges at Roath • Battle of the Severn Sabrina Afon Hafren

Historians

Historians' output has increased
is increasing
a strict regimen might save us
ought to be diminished
corpulence useless
threatens the vital organs
much of it waste.

A strict regimen
and ought to be diminished
vulgarisations bloat bookshelves
threaten the vital organs
hypertrophy with learning
of learning with hypertrophy
of bookshelves with bloat
much of it is corpulence.

Academic fat clogs the bibliographies
and threatens the vital corpulence
is increasing and ought and otherwise
much of it imposes a starvation
much of it a strict taxpayer
ought to be bloat.

Revolted by the useless corpulence
we need much of it
writers who take pride and
writers who take pride and
writers who waste
patrons and taxpayers
and vulgarisations
Academic fat clogs the bloat
strict history ought to float

We need much of it
vital historians' corporations
taxpayers, bibliographies,
learned bookshelves and bloat
writers who take pride and
ought to be diminished

the bloat and the vulgarisations
writers who take pride and
reviewers who take prisoners
writers who take pride and
reviewers who take prisoners
writers who take pride and
reviewers who take prisoners
writers who take pride and
reviewers who take prisoners
writers who take pride and
reviewers who take prisoners
writers who take pride and
reviewers who take prisoners
writers who take pride and
reviewers who take books

Much of it is waste
the historians ought the they then
slipshod
oh yes apoplexy
and how they
clog clog and bloat

The output they h'm
might might might
slip sl
The historians then will be vital
increase increased the they them
the historians
will write about it
yes they will.

Dw'i ddim yn deall

❄👇✋💧 ✋💧❄👇

☜ 🕈✌✡ ✋❄☝

🏳☜💧 ☠🏳🕈 ✌

☠👎 🏳☠

Software

wiredkick soft hotass ware beautiful user makes
soft beautiful user kickwired wareass makes hot
beautiful kickware softass makes user hot wired
kickuser beautiful ware makes asssoft wired hot
assware beautiful kickhot soft user makes wired
beautiful hotass makes usersoft wired ware kick
hotmakes beautiful kick ware wired softuser ass
wiredass user ware makes hot soft hot hot kick
kickwired softhot hot hot hot hot hot hot hotass
ass hot kick hot hotware makes soft ass hot hot
ass kick makes beautiful user hotware softwired
ware makes beautiful user hotwired asskick soft
hot wired kickass software makes user beautiful
$49.50 download today

Fix-up

Mabinogion Translations

He made for the court in the court he could
aye said Pwll to the court the court and they spent
maiden wilt   whatever boon
the court hosts and dominions
what is here? a badger a court
the men of the court to feel heaviness
awoke born lady not the court the chamber
at the door lo a horse court here the wld
court catch you fix-up bile racially
the court crt cart will repay thee raised fit
daughter gwyn gohoyw ap gloyw wally lydan
ap casnar court wledig seisyllwch of the high branch rit
mst grac graze nn mor morrow th tend tenderness
the diz ss till there affection affection retinue
rrr llll land

Rev (again)

In (of)
promontory
point
away
glimpsed g
he's blots
for r
of Oriel
(bird, fish, glass, donkey)
articles
for I'm
from
well shame shame
most islands
it
ping
useful
(Body, Polley, Dworkin, Malin, Misanthropy,
Diatribe, Arbitary, Body Rub, Weather Front)
and
before cation garde
real
personally of ion tion
(let down, let out, let anyway)
any
two
on on m
screen n
men you men
if have the
on
even doing
are
ironic elderly helped
when
memory she

love
stands
the just
the
with memory
wrote uch itchgaps
slow
ther theo
cept barriers
begins begins
begins ings
a single sheet
a listen euphony
a crack shft
a pressure dr
a poetr tensio
finch finch finch finch
finch finch finch finch
finch finch finch finch
finch finch finch finch
finch finch finch finch
finch finch finch finch
finch finch finch finch
finch finch finch finch
finch finch finch finch
finch finch finch finch
finch finch finch finch
finch finch finch finch
finch finch finch finch
finch finch finch finch
finch finch finch finch
finch finch finch finch
finch finch finch finch
finch finch finch finch
finch finch finch finch
finch finch finch finch
finch finch finch finch
finch finch finch finch
finch finch finch finch

finch finch finch finch
finch finch finch finch
finch finch finch finch
finch finch fnich fissh
finch finch finch finch
finch finch finch finch
finch finch finch finch
finch finch finch finch
finch finch finch finch
finch finch finch finch
finch finch finch finch
finch finch finch finch
finch finch finch finch
finch finch finch finch
finch finch finch finch
finch finch finch finch
finch finch finch finch

deception

lost

doesn't much mat
who re
any

missing sections: eptive, ad, way, ocked, lettes, letter, listener, letterer.

Cover Blown

In Memoriam William Burroughs

William Burroughs goes to Rio
for a new face. It's a brilliant piece of
plastic surgery, makes him look
like a taller JFK. He's so proud getting
off the airliner at New York's Dextromorphine
that the bullet coming at him
smiles a little itself before going in.
It makes shotgun art on the 747's side.
Could have been anyone
Burroughs's mouth says while
his Brooks' suit body slumps el
hombre invisible cover blown.
In Lawrence, Kansas when John F
finally slides into the earth the West
thinks it's lost a city in the red night.
And it has.

Once You Know Where To Point

I'm falling through the door
at high pressure and not
stopping to do anything but
check the light on the answerphone.
The high heat of the yard the tubs needing
gallons at least the hallway has
a trail of leaf-flakes like bits of skin.
I can feel the damp in my lower back
grow up a map of India.
I work the oven with its
roaring fan and gargled heat.
There are no spaces anywhere
but the past. Burroughs took
his future into the garden and
shot-gunned it faster than de Kooning.
"Once you know where to point,
all you have to do is get out of the way
and let this thing happen."
In the dark later I collect the cybertrash
from the system and it's there, folded-in,
about a half line long.
El hombre Invisible now invisible.
In a way always was.

Pantycelyn: The Tools & Things Version

(after D Gwenallt Jones)

Aaa aa aa aaaa aaaa'a aaaa, aaaaaa a Aaa,
Aa aa aa aaaaa aarr rr Rrrrrr Rrrr,
Rr rrrrrr rrrrrrrr Rr Rrrrreeeee Ee
Ee eeeee eeeeeee ee Eeee eeeeeii iii:
Iiiiii ii Iiiiii ii Ii iiiii, i'i iyyyy
Yy yyyy yyyyy'y yyyyy y'y yyy y'y yywww,
Ww ww Ww Wwww Ww www, Ww wwwww d'd dddd
D dddd, d dddd dddd dddd d nnnn.
Gwniadur, teipiadur, berwedydd, pibell,
ysgrafell, melin, cribin, clustog, bidog,
crafwr, tynnwr, golchwr, gobennydd, dysychydd
N nnnnnnn, n nnnnnnnn nngg g ggggg,
Ggg ggggg gttt t tttt, tttt ttttt lll,
Llllll, ll ll looooooooo, ooo offfff
F ffffff dd ddddddddd dddd d Ddddd,
D'c cccc ccc ccss ssss s ssshhh h hhhu
U'u uuuu ubbb bbccchchc hchm mmrhrh âââff Llp.

Wonderful Life

N rth f R g rst n   n th
cnl beet f th Seerh wy Vll y
EE w nd r why th h us s bckeeng
 nt thees lg flytra c l brt
 utd r leef   weeth a rwonderful lifen nt
brbee s nd xt nseev atee s nt
wheech th dreezzl flls t th
Reeseeng Sun n sun veeseebl b cus   f
nveel h d cuwonderful lifeulee ath g s
ua thr ugh th b g l f wonderful life uld f
C d WONDERFUL LIFEwr w ds
und r wheech W lsh Wt r r r uteeng
 wonderful lifeeen dreen g ug th tr s
dr a th y ll w aeea stuff eet ll
bck h a ll thees f r fst r sheet
b y nd lee s WONDERFUL LIFEyn dd WONDERFUL LIFEch n
rdee wonderful lifest nd brck n theen
wonderful lifen swonderful life keeng weeth gr yh und
d thees n xt.

A t r Feench

A t r Feench, 19 S uthwonderful lifeeenst r R d, R th, Crdeeff CF2 5T

Philip Larkin

Ted Hughes' animals
not to unwrap the parcel critic on their
being which is not Philip Larkin give them
something all signifier a world not to
be done all in order to deanaesthetized three
exalted parcel throw away the package just
another he wants will gradually realise
the theorists dull and exalted solved and
almost but never quite has nothing like
Seamus into being which is not
frustrated and angry except its own
works re-realise in English terms very
effective serious jumping up and down
will recur among the theorists of the bog
people bedsits in particular the power is
not what is demanded of the parcel since it
is an ancient thing innate with new alternatives
nothing inside but expository unwrapped
approval of a few powers signifier signified
with inbuilt flaws which are not the world
of the bedsits which is why Larkin is
not like Ted Hughes not like Ted Hughes at all.

Sophistication

When J showed me how it could be done I took it as natural this was the way. You walk into your father's shop your father has one you are rich smile at the assistant behind the counter staring vacantly into her Daily Mirror reach below the Max Factor rack pull the concealed nail from the side of the wooden cash-drawer lift forty white fivers slick and fast. J told me he was fucking the assistant but he didn't say where. At the steak bar he sent the wine back corked I didn't drink any even when the good bottle arrived. J showed me lots of things four dozen air-brushed Harrison Marks and his sister pissing his dog with a hard-on how to start a car without keys. The dentist's daughter sitting in the park lunch-time he fucked her too money buys you sophistication we passed her she didn't even look up. Great life. Eventually J went to Australia for £10 after five cars ended in streams and trees his fingerprints on them or seen doing it his father told me I was a nice lad he was sorry his sister didn't flicker J fucked her too he said she was a real sport really keen. I got to know that myself later. Received one postcard no picture said Kalgoorlie was dusty but things were looking up could I send him some cash I didn't. Nothing at all after that.

newjobs

varnish remover

dadaboxer

jocyr gwyddelig

high roller

dutch nude

haddock fürer
(easier than Lavazza)

dolig sodder

arte povera[1]

free sandwiches

sponsor davies

gwatsiwch fan hyn

[1] default position

Hey Baby

in the dark maybe baby the touch rich enough
rough encrusted in dreams we walk my hand
in yours mouth sweet enough little baby blue
full of peach down smelling of lava rush
dust sandstorm blossom petunia stamen honey
rose flash petal-water blow froth foam
I am the one I am the one hush.
You can fall in love as many times as you like
sky on fire, all that roaring, million songs
and in the dark who cares. Rocking robin
luscious lips hit me hit me hey baby.
But try the cold light. Try it then.
I put Frank back on the player
so achingly old fashioned.
There you go, lady lay,
out through the door.

Wobble

oulipienne oscillatory

Rain drought water deserter
Growth shrinkage engorgement puke
coal newspaper newspaper newspaper
curry feather heated night-time
Gower bollock peninsular whoppa
minister fish faith internet

health fatboy insurance Cardi
class solo committee sheep
burger windfarm wallet mouth
poem bongo argument document
peace prick lie-down thunderstorm
Llyn Grangetown pencil Harry Ramsden's

Say birdcage diatribe foreigner
Glass borough vinyl missionary
Duw fatboy Mendelssohn slice-up
Artist vote certificated loopy
Money rain coupon crisp-packet
Sheep sheep sheep sheep

No Bike

I have been speaking at my door with the distraught woman who has let her daughter go lost. I am playing Mendelssohn's Violin Concerto in here and feel like I am gliding up a highway in the sun. The woman says her child — you know her, the one with the pink bike and its little outriders — was in the park, went to the park, peddled past here, came up this road, along this path, this way, you saw her smiling, you did. I have been deep in the music and my head full of wide spaces I tell her I have not I am sorry I shake my head. The woman has on a white blouse with a button missing and straggle hair that's been clipped ragged where it brushes her chest. Her shoes are flat and their leather is scratched. She twists her hands into each other. She looks back. Along the road there is no girl, no bike. I can't tell her anything. She has brown arms and a bangle. She'll turn up. I was with Mendelssohn. The street is hot. The music soared. She is burning, this woman. Her face is melting. All of it, it's coming off. For comfort I remind myself that in other places across the world there are worse fears in the faces of the destitute and the dying. Worse than this. I look at the woman again. Long and slow. No, right now, there are not.

Zen Cymru

Abereiddy !
Ah, Abereiddy, ah !
Abereiddy, ah !

The beginning of autumn
Sea and sea and sea
All the same

eeeeeeee eeeeeee
eeeeeeee eeeeeeee
eee eeeeees

ssss sssssssssss
sssss sss sssssss
sss sssssssee

Could be moon
Out there
Who cares

No more thunder
Hear hard belching
Outside the pub

By a cottage collapsed
Are men
Thinking of money

These sheep
So happy
How do you know they are not?

The stars speak so loud
In the Preseli blackness
It's just rain

Light over Trefdraeth
Behind the clouds
Then clear

The days go cold
And I am still in my khaki
Peg pants

This Wales leaks there isn't one
That doesn't
Is there?

Splottlands !
Ah Splottlands, ah !
Ah, Splott !

Tree looks like wind
Wave is moon spirit
Wrecked car what we do

On the great gable porch of
St John the Baptist Sikh glory
The butterfly bush still blooms

In this vast Wales you must not help yourself to any
meadow, flower or rockoutcrop that belongs to another.
Mountains, springs, the peat wildernesses all have an owner;
be careful about this.

Go out and you meet yourself
Come home
And you're still there

Is that the cloud moving?
Maybe
So what

On the headland
Do not speak
This is such a virtue

R S was once asked by an acolyte
"What is the meaning of the thin tongue inheriting the universe?"
R S answered
"The mangels in the fields below the hills"

If you know, you don't speak
If you babble, you have no idea
We are a nation of noisy bastards

The sea darkens
You can see the small boats dumping oil drums
By the light of the stars

Sea
Ahh eeeeee
Ahh eeeeee

Saunders wrote, he could have done:
poems and science are opposed,
the former purposing immediate pleasure, unlike the
latter which is a hunt for truth.

Red face
In the endless field
Then back to the tractor

Going to Paradise is good, and to fall into Hell also is a matter of congratulation. Old Buddha by the Golden Road in the rocks of Foel Trigairn. Still invisible.

The ships pass but make no move to leave their reflection,
the sea makes no effort to hold how they look.
The clouds drift
it is spring, it is autumn..

They are young people. Though they are not
drunk they still wreck the station and
are sick before the passengers.

"But what am I to do?" said Alice. "Anything you like."
said the footman, and began whistling.

We hear the tune, you and I,
but inside our ears it is always a different one.

Rainfall

constant

Putting In The Window

(after Tom Leonard)

Glazunov's Double Concerto
Mozart's C minor Glazing Bar

INTERVAL

Rossini's Stabat Drip Strip
Mendelssohn's Violin Serenade in Soft Putty

Encore: Mahler's Tenth Lintel

Paint

Violent White
Azure Eyepatch
Winter Arse
Gurgling Sands
Underarm Crush
Blueberry Sandinista
Tropical Testosterone
Sunkist Yellow Underpant
Vanilla Vertigo
Mango Vagina
Warm Topsoil
Duodenum Jade
Fresh Acne

What is the maximum number of times
you have had to repaint the
wall below the dado?

Seven.

Rhai Caneuon Cymraeg

Os gallaf helpu rhywun

Disgyblion Iesu Grist

Er cof am fuwch o'r enw Molly

Cowboi bach tŷ ni

Dos draw Moses

Lisa lân

Caru Cymru

Titw Tomos las

Llongau Caernarfon

Pentre bach Llanber

Hen Feibl Mamgu

Dyma gariad fel y moroedd

My Hen laid a haddock

F'anwylyd f'anwylyd

Hen lwybr y mynydd

Cofio o hyd

Iesu Iesu rwyt ti'n ddigon ("Clawdd Madog")

Beth sydd o'i le

Un fendith dyro im ("Bo Diddley")

Gwely gwag

'Sdim eisiau dweud ffarwel

Hei Ho Noni No

Slingwr gwn ydy Meic Stevens

Mae'r llais yn galw

Gymru lân gwlad y gân

Gymru lân gwlad y two tongues

Gymru lân gwlad y bobl mewn oed

Gymru lân hand in the till

No arabs in Blaenau Ffestiniog ("Land of Hope and Glory")

Seren seren pull a fish from your bottom

Y deryn du a'i blufyn sidan

Ffidl ffadl

Titrwm tatrwm

Totrwm tylli tô

Rhwng Bethesda a'r groes (Cymysgiad clwb)

Y Bugail Tonyrefail

Blow The Wind Southerly

Rhondda Is Where My Heart Is

Swing That Hammer (Cân Serch)

Swing That Hammer (fersiwn R.S.Thomas)

Swing That Hammer (Meredydd Evans a'i fand)

Ei di'r deryn du?

Porthcawl Co-operative Society Rock n Roll Mambo

Once More With Feeling

Yn boeth fel tân

That's enough

The Unstoppable Growth of British Leyland

This accounts for a fifth
of all British trees. Pensioners
are concerned about their ceilings. "Yes, dear".
The Residential Hedgerow Bill will
vigour. Hybrid th. I have
delivered my eulogy. My telescopic
shear and platform. The covenants are sss sig.
High Hedges vs. the ban expect advice
and leaflets. Layla leylandii.
Wind filter flower pariah
break pollution bishop Welshpool
nootkatensis clone pitbull brother
dark volley henchman viagra
Would Hampton Court Assgrow
Conifer shear Conifer Conif?
Yes they would.

Quantum Mechanics
in the work of R S Thomas

Reciprocities
turning
large affirmation
inexplicable
dominant identity
destiny
intimate hearing
memoriam
velocity
reading book
cricket bat
lean owl
exaggerated crag
sheaf
simulacrum
stuffed turkey
ethos
throughout monotony denouement
blood
sky blood
all blood
sky skeleton frequencies
hide hiding hidden

select winner from list:
Joseph Conrad; Jacques Derrida; H.J.Blackham;
Ludwig Wittgenstein; Baruch Spinoza; C Norris

veal
blood
memorial philosophy particle probable
sheaf of poems
so large you wonder

argument ambiguity
age
butter

Mid Period Anglo-Welsh Endings

(with Loan Word Intrusions)

ove ing es ly ed od ing ic ing ing
orrow ing ing ies ing ing ing ed
ing ing ents ows ly ing ing es
ills ent ough ing ing or or ow
er er er ed er er er er er ert er
ing ing ed ing ing ing ess ed
ills ing ing ing ed ed ing ings
ight ted erns ed oor ly ly ly
edourd ies ound ions ed ing
ent ing ness ent ing ould ly
ince ing ing ing ing ed ings
ic al eat ince ince ing ed ed ed
ers ed ed ing ills ars ible ed

Taff Llandough Gwydion Ianto
Ceridwen Blodeuwedd Cariad Hanes
Arglwyddi Fferyllt da Prydain
Culhwch Olwen Cantref Sion crying Daro
Cwm Cadno Llanrhaedr-ym-Mochnant
Tywysog Tal Tal Tal Tal Tal Tal Tal Tyddyn
Glyndwr Llewelyn Fawr Deganwy
Aberffraw Cynon Dyffryn
Caersalem Pantycelyn
Iago Iago mangle-juice hills

ing ied ul er ed ing an ore an arly
ly ue urn ew ing ead oads ey eak
ing ing ing sts ing ind ad ed ing
ing ing id ied er er ed ing ing
ing ing ing ing ing ing ing ing ulser ed
est enly et ed ains irs ing
ed ed ess lds ed ains irs ing
ing oom ing ed oom ed oom aws
ence ed ed ed ing ing ily
ed ed ed ion ed ed ed other
other oom oom other oom other

SNT no 18

SICT 2ASD?
TAML &MT
RWDS TDBOM
&SLH A2SAD8
S2HTE OHS
&OIHGCD
&EFFF SD
BCON CCU
BTES SNF
NLP OTFTO
NSDB TW'stIHS
WIEL 2TTG
 SL AMCB OECS
 SL LS &TGLTT

Slide Guitar Devices

10.10 am

bleach off the debris

glass

Was

slide guitar devices:
            neck of Beck
            steel comb
            lipstick

Hooker never did this
just the
            paddle
and
the rhythmic drm

Does

            it ever last?
the moment
when the Zip is full

erase

erase

            don't

How Things Break Down

the dynamic always moves towards entropy

        leaf fibre
        coat distress
        paper sponge
        64-mil hard sized
        staple rust

went up the ladder gale shirt balloon
fast set cement tub warm wtr pointing trowel
third time in two decades
scrape and grit the 1927 black mortar out in a
grey rain wash put it back.

        skin slough
        love two-stroke
        stitch gap
        cold sore
        need need not want

Conscious

move the chi
by
sending the left temporal lobe to the centre
(tan tien) (heat source) (real seat) (no mind)
catch and push off

goes

        pin ball
        lariat
        leaf

        voice
                unblocks
        the gates

zoom

did this in the bookshop
two shelves, that's 324 volumes, some substantial,
in the air,
one go, one hand.

I think I'll Go Hunt Bears

complexity — one of the
sleepwalking cinnabar
loose alliance, interchange
fleshy babies
scratching figures
does not totter
the mix of myth & sociopolitical

shadow

explain
Explain

shadow

there is usually no way to know in
advance where any given atom might be found
in an unknown crystal structure. A structure
solution can take weeks. Shift the
dirt with bleach soak overnight then
gone or ghost. when you look faint maybe.
these things
only do what they do when you watch
no spirit without passion   no love in a vacuum
no soul in the heights no sex w/out film

all the shadow is:

45
teeth electricity
ley
misremember
chip
line of soap
mark

The Code

sleep

space

need

final

The Glow

Clouds harvest stone moorland
Memory bones bracken fluttering
Baubles cowries rulers sunlight
God furrows worship tremble
Nothing fountain bitter flowers
Obstinacy gorging counsellors running
Weakness stubborn dark artificer

Nucleus religion charmer bacteria
Drowned suppurate fractured water
Idiot orchestra idiot laughter
Mangle departure death dreamer
Chaucer Pope Wales England
God hills quilts gardens
Hair men art comfort
Rig window rain-hammered dazzle

Gold conviction land light
Language music haunted stillness
Dance dust rafter flower
Gorse gyre halo breaking
Leaves sleep singing endless

tick in box

Abse	☐
Clarke	☐
Curtis	☐
Davies	☐
Fisher	☐
Jenkins	☐
Jenkins	☐
Jenkins	☐
Jones	☐
Jones	☐
Jones	☐
Jones	☐
Jones	☐
Lewis	☐
Mills	☐
robson	☐
Thomas	☐
Thomas	☐
Williams	☐

Pitt Rivers

is dark   th cases of pipes,
money, knives, mojo,
game, hair grip,
dolls, paper, fire makers,
charm, mirror, club,
I pass. Pause at
the Polynesian island map
split bamboo, cowry,
twine. Stop by the
drawers of voodoo doll,
pins, powerless here,
like badly made toys.
Examine with a torch the
General's obsession.
Magic. How we make the
world do what we want.
Bundle placed in the
spring to lay a curse on the
village. It consists of:
1.The hair of the witch who
used it.
2. Earth from the grave of a
man killed by a tiger.
3. Earth from the grave of a
woman who died in childbirth
4. Two leaves of a tree axumia
which withers quickly
5. Piece of a giant plant an
irritant if eaten.
6. A nettle
7. Leaf of a tree which sheds
its leaves in the heat.
Rengma, Tesophenyu Village,
Naga Hills. Looks like
dried shit. The General
down the well
in his hat.
Didn't die.
Not yet.

How To Speak (1)

th thin gr w n th p p the m s c's p d f r w p t n ll th w rk
l rning j st wh m c s ds ke m k ing r m hs m ve t. t pls
anyway. Th tr I th yar is there thw ck ing s ss ss sssss on
the ss g ing ggr rght tps wnt rr rr sssss didn't it th th l
spr c t th sc sss fol not ocked ack fr st lik r v ices w h
v to sp kk sss we sing n t n m ng w d an w ww sss sss
ss ave to 's h m n c nd t d w g t sal ere? ss ss ssss n the
ar th e g t th r rd m ch n n t lo d l sss ndd dd ask what
next. dr nk. sss ss go home.

e oe ou ea a e e i i ueo e oe oa aye e ee i ao iia aaua you o
ey a i oo i' o u a ae o ea ea a ea ae o ueai ie ie yeo aii o e a
e you o' exe e. ee' a i aou ee e euie a a u o o a u a o, o a ie
i ou ay oo I' i oo oy e oe' ae a a ou o u oey e ou ee a uy
aeie e i ey ae e o ie. a ex. o ou o.

How To Speak (2)

these things grow on
they push up
the music's paid for
we've put in all this work
learning just what music sounds like
making our mouths move
to it. It plays anyway.
The tree in the yard is there
thwacking its fronds on the glass
getting bigger bright tips
winter didn't stop it these
the blue spruce toothed scale
foliage not knocked back
by frost like our voices
we have to speak we sing
no tune no timing we do
anyway we have to it's a
human condition do
we get salary here? In the
bar they've got the record
machine on too loud lean in
and ask what next. drink.
go home.

we open our
heads and let the light in
surgeons help Homer
Thomas Carlyle the Green
Knight Carlos Williams
Zarathustra you know
they can sing too it's
not just a matter of search
beams and great splashes of
understanding brightness
like yellow paintings on
the wall when you don't expect
them. There's a thing about
these new centuries that wants

us to own as much as know,
to tag life with our spray
logo I'm with sloop doggy
he doesn't care a damn bout
fronds just money
get out there and buy batteries
then find they are the wrong
size. What next. Mr Spock
would know.

Slow To Change

Boundless

sea billowing sky idle water supplication patience scorn beseeming bowers slaughtered saints lyre organ breaths Alpine mountain victory monarch shore heart weep heaven beauty liquefaction glitter loyalty wanton liberty woodland courtesy lilac fallen star shoreward wind rose cool deep leaf narrow bed gay northern lights watch-dogs moss owl feather sheaves rounded cheeks vestige leaves bewildering bower springtide church dove yew stable misty solitudes linnet poor song endure grim forge hoar frost patience behold the vapour weep heaven's gates russet gorse knoll rejoice countenance kind pity strong patience earth blind ordinance foolish tears clamorous wings Solomon Maud Hester Rosabelle grief woeful conceit withering heath dear dead summer sands of time lent pine eternal sight light twixt childhood graves and bones heedless sons foreboding tears patience steeple water wan cheek deliverance fidelity truth patience blessed victory might gallantry majesty certainty death atonement patient breath sky tearful joy victorious bower blessed air

Fast

loose toast desiccated hills red cloud refuge phosphorescent trail void point agitation tumour work-lust narcotic faith suck fright gravity burnt-out hotel sunlit mnemonic sparse foliage good faith technician flavour stain detritus jet tramp motorway bloodshot trolley shard pasta knuckle Venus quenched quail saltpetre patina lingering infestation gull support affection snake ochre white crossroad Marbella Beryl Babel babble broom mop fruit terrorist capitalist dream cord semantic trigger totem tarmac trap bird gear smouldering lavender-blue seal canker crisp inkstain shed speech bracken bullshit dishevelled dry high wire smoke dreg carbohydrate fluffball keyhole virus psychopath knackered outrage tart outrider torch social path render reflect wreck azure slippery monochrome calf coconut vicious branch tight hard scorn whiplash seaweed municipality baffle breath camphire barrow left linger lost lamented lingering wrench earthlight bayleaf stasis body weight shift water truck engineered fish damp lime splinter flash fiction clarity victim naked truth work corrugated cladding

Easy X-Rays

Euclidean
ethyl ether
Clouet
Bulwer-Lytton
dentifrice
Lagomorpha
Aberystwyth
Chungking
quibbles
Han Cities
treacherous
calc-
deposited
rotundus
antennae
sodium lamp
oculomotor
nerve
tussle
imprecise
meridiem
waxiest
Aveyron
Indonesia.
debris
glucosuria
fishnet
cooking.Assam
Carl
self-fertlizing
Sabbaths
forestall
life-support
grouped.
Shivers
Sapiens
timbers
S.C.M.
Lithospermum
heaven
apomict
electoral college
Panax
review copy
lairy

Caquet
stereospecific
catalyst
mammae
mortis
doloroso
Harrisburg.
kier
scrollwork
silo
field emission
bad-mannered
blood bank
turtle.
compendium
mullet
Jos''ephine
validity.
foots
fraternal
no-nonsense.
Vergilius
over-optimistic
concession.
lickspittle
cobalt bomb
tantalite
pollard
Vibrio
Philosophia
hammering
Newham
feaze
improper
integral
Hsinking
dulcis
heptameter
vestrymen
mangabey
fricandeau
objectivity
-art
D.H.
steadfastness

Arras
Adenauer
gracioso
standoffish
Giotto
micrometer
screw
Antarctic
Peninsula
readiest
metathorax
Andreotti
dachshund
slight
inhibiting
Verdun
air scoop
Zamboanga
spread-eagle
wrestler's
Holy Island
Jotunheim
sullen
self-sealing
False Bay
Omagh.
circuit breaker
joke
diplomatics
bield
exalting
law-abiding
buttock
zoometry
simoom
insult
NH2C6H4COOH
keep back
semiotics
charas
circumstantial
Styx
romance.
Fs
numerable

control chart
disarming
titillating
cabbages
comparisons
quasi-contract
pine cone
Dies
keel.
predestine
myel-
adobe
Berber
calla
kist
Lester
billyo
aegis
monk.As
Myliobatidae
scientifically
thyroideus
surrendered.
old-fashioned
doable
herbivorous
sidesman
overproduction
superego
Cornish pasty
loblolly
conformist
crosstree
Jazz
matins
fountain
unctuous
Lammastide
bozo
monogamist
head voice
constringe
lawns.
Father
Christmas

artifact
gauzier
Brussel
casing
handcraft
Dafydd
Ferdinand I
burweed
Magnificent
adit
wheelwright
mortifying
Zanzibar
gyve
aviate
febri-
fishwife
lentil
parramatta
intolerably
Lisboa
suffocating
pummel
Lepontine Alps
fire hydrant
nonmusical
alpestrine
tannage
colossus
burrows
re-present
Citizens'
Boswell's
resolute
homily
full-size
vertebra
cakes.
P.L.A.
drupes
methyl chloride
namas
cold shoulder
flavicepshaving
legal tender
perfunctory
patriarchate
gee
Fructidor
Titoism
waterside
organoleptic
disulphide.
swamps
aud.
Cathar
mothproof
noughts and
crosses
silk-lined
Justinianus.
alee
North Island
flatterer
Ephraimite
orle
rock-crushers
Platanaceae.
Philippine Sea
couching
bats-in-the-
belfry
contracture
Ekaterinodar
hopper
Runner
hhd
nonsense verse
Chiclayo
Hama
Altai Mountains
putty-like
joinery
Arries
Nanking.
rye bread
autopilot
Boreal
skimpier
subdivided
natural history
Sultan
CDT
airier
dodgy
balalaika
Dust
Piedmont
cryogenics
vaunt-courier
tracheitis
tasteful
Bernhard
Vincent's
limit man
muscleman
microscopical
Colbert
catchy
Welsh dragon
fridgemagnet
Ingul
Gettysburg
sesquicarbonate
Delaunay
half-hardy
goggle
side-dress
fulgurant
Cinderella
theophany
shuteye
Scopus
Dutch elm
disease
spelk
reeve
contrail
binder
Hospitalet
cruentus
barrier
greatness
Crucible
prepositions
Calcarius
four-poster
ball-like
Etruscans
diviner
copyrighted
subordinating
oblique-angled
controversial
Armoric
Nagyvarad
Assets
unloose
Heliozoa
scutch
grunting
2Ni
collective
security
Chartism
methought
adamant
Fe2SiO4
John Osmond
Perchlorate
Pyrochroa
radiolocation
riata
overspend
C5H10O4
environmental
prophecy
molybdous
silversides
stringhalt
Port Louis
Taxus
records.
refrigerated
haemolysin
belittled
clairvoyance
howl down
longitude
instructs
Aethusa
affords
hued
sprag
Viridiana
Mayo.
Ghost
liberties
surfers
vireo
rivalry.
plasmagenes
Swan
Tungting.
dinner.Austral.
well-founded

cuvieri
trifolia
glycolic
lengthened
Dezhnev
Cranach
latex
Tyrone.
war baby
Coppelia
Koko
Dragoons
god.
volution
latter
encasing
drunkenly
Crookes tube
hussar
disentitle
btry.
curly-coated
cease-fire
baro-
flashlight
boatswain's
unquestionably
gingerly
scapular
antitussive
lysimeter
last.on
cross-bench
sure-fire
Nuremberg
oestriol
citified
justificatory
squint-eyed
shouldst
luciliae
reserved
allergen
Icelandic
lavolta
CaNaK
dyer's-weed
salaries
gopher

demodulation
Father's Day
stumpier
cuculiform
inalterable
identical
Venetic
convex
leanings
Warszawa
zoochore
pentlandite
standover
inactively
Mohandas
score
zayin
Milne
cerebro-
price
discrimination
whiskers
tetracid
padauk
bane
spermatic cord
transmuting
Leiria
colcannon
remarque
Roubaix
Wattenscheid
Kuznetsk
royal icing
Cavalier
selenide.
Seaton Valley
acre
arraigned
wrier
Deep
babbitt
fieri facias
jackpot
subjective
idealism
burke
bastard measles
deflected

Teleprompter
chalcid
half-breed
corslet.
Archipielago
Oh
contexture
clavicle
-carp
unaccountably
countries.U.S.
clams
tempter
twilled-silk
pence
Duque de Caxias
encounter
oversensitive
Roost
freezing works
Americus
wallpaper
Heracleum
dramatized
Karlsruhe
Yoknapatawpha
indefinite
snakelike
unlearned
kreutzer
booted
smeared
Urania
phylloxera
episcopate
C.D.
winged
Albino
preach
perish.
slippy
lexicon
muscid
Charollais
doing
bulwarks
veneered
goodwife
sceptically

Leibnitz.
Hauts-de-Seine
Pausanias
entails
RCB
volt.
stigmasterol
Elaeagnus
pensionable
capsule
Lucas
terrestial
Roche-sur-Yon.
Blimp
Sarum
earthworks
stercorarius
regelation
tin-opener
Citrus
tortuous
windcheater
lochia
Lanius
kerchief
hobnail
prospectors
upswept
ganoin
recursion
derisive
penthouse
metheglin
gypsy moth
pewee
Novocaine
Latin alphabet
resolutive
Reuben
Satureja
bestead
reticule
ugly duckling
Kiangsu.
algebraic
being.
State
platen
motion

impregnated
liberal arts
Tobit
coumarin
Pentecost
perm
hampers
Bougainvillea
Dauda
Lawrence.
tulip-like
credit standing
fluke
Llanystumdwy
governments.
dentures
Beaverboard
remonstrant
bracer'2
coefficients
happenstance
jellied
barrow boy
Laodicea
rettos
pileate
parget
onions.
insubordination
reproof
magistrate
pinching
Diels-Alder
NCH3CH2COOH
praemunire
firemen
elfland
joggle
saiga
jewellery
rhythm
onus probandi
Diels-Alder
NCH3CH2COOH
praemunire
firemen
elfland
joggle
saiga

diatropic
UNCTAD
pepper mill
RP
drawknife
Satyricon
Renate
Rowan
inspan
Almera
biochemical
Livorno
stewardess
3-ply
complete
emus
guidebook
aucuparia
unprofitable
sectorial
parasitic
intermittent
claudication
Botaurus
distort
enamel-like
sclerotomy
lacklustre
Percheron
clinches
waste
Thomism
scuttlebutt
landmasses
dendrite
Bazett
glows
unexceptional
Ipomoea
entity
Workingmen's
saprobe
dendrite
Bazett
glows
unexceptional
Ipomoea
entity
Workingmen's

landlord
antinode
1b.
Agaricus
Bragg's law
tunnel disease
dolore
Baikal
extern
Lorient
Dicaeidae
hallucination
cleaning
walk
datary
telly
danger
lamb's lettuce
formal
trapezoid
charterer
dishcloth
astound
me.And
deodorize
educate
pauper
dhuti
Myrica
Ibbetson
dyestuff
alpha ray
alling sickness
Nottinghamshire.
Ocypus
expected value
Boru
ideaimpulsive
pigswill
chasseur
comique
young lady
Ocypus
expected value
Boru
idea
impulsive
pigswill
chasseur

natans
gullibility
cordon bleu
parrot
caballus
Celtiberian
Rumpelstiltskin
Curtailment
Middle-aged
sock away
Vanya
chromonema
dilations
radical axis
penna
billet
wood ibis
unreplaceable
Mycostatin
old bird
malignant
Kurgan
two-foot
leg bye
waxberry
yellow-white
cattery
A.E.
Jeans
approximately
cithara
pinchpenny
fancy man
waste
ludovicianus
spear side
Berlin
thorough brace
cleidoic egg
Ingres
Behar.
coumarone
spear side
Berlin
thorough brace
cleidoic egg
Ingres
Behar.
coumarone

jewellery
rhythm
onus probandi
tones.
Little England
Ru
Burseraceae
Botany wool
linguistics
weather-resistant
striae
Tallahassee
Mustafa Kemal
Beyond Wales
scurrying
Passion
waste
enthralled
Iron Chancellor
revere
riband
Bill.
discloses
poll tax
isocyanic
longshore drift
scleroderma
Chronicle
edaphic
pyrosis

saprobe
ostracods
Clive
skid
quartern
simulate
Boudicca
attempts
pannikin boss
cold sweat
Kodaly
crystalline
levies
antiperspirant
Index
Ketch
brig
Boileau-
Despreaux.
restructuring
nicotinamide
bolivar.
totalizer
plonifolia
catboat
Mond process
disconcerted
Grand
hayrack
Athena

comique
young lady
historical
linguistics
year
distributee
pa’anga.
lopho-
Rogers
tittup
knoll
claws
long-period
footslog
m.s.l.
LiAlSi2O6
term
reed bunting
ptero-
water thrush
Aythya
Maccabaeus
omitted.
Peter.
asphodel
men
pleo-
solvolysis
thalassocracy
waist

cloth
Henze
hoofs
germinal vesicle
Easy
Not easy
Urinogenital
See earlier
Much earlier
Most of life
whisky mac
Sporades
waste
waste
waste
waste
waste
waste
waste
waste
waste
waste
waste
waste
waste
waste
waste
waste
waste
waste

Llywarch Hen SMS with fault

DK b4Dyln's hall 2nite
no flr no bd
i wp wp – o o o

line 1 eto
no flr no ^ ^ ^
save GD – sane how ????

dd b4dyln hrd rck
roof xx sais bstd
GD w?

nt ovr bones f b4dylan
nt yet ~ ~

Chaos Theory

Living things are in a constant state of organised flux – growing, jamming, switching, revising, bottling, eczema-growing, inhaling – a condition that runs against the move to stasis, everything shifts to where movement is unnecessary, least resistance, softest energy, flow by gravity, slow (argument in pub — what is entropy: disorder or silence. I favour the cessation of particle movement, gaps between, cold. Others insist chaos. Diversion to discover burning iron weighs more after the fire than before. Soul leaving the body in a flame of belief. Corpse accumulates. Small whiskeys arrive.) Everything does not draw to a state of shapeless disorder. Inanimate wears. Steps have the shape of feel. Chairs. Pathways. Door jams. Head rests. Form last refuge. Turing: The chemical basis of morphogenesis, math simulates reaction-diffusion, don't look to explain, to find the traces of god in the distant signatures of light. Instead, in the chemical soup. These shapes in the mist. These new ghosts. Before ghosts. No sign in the formulae. Nothing on the x-ray. No sightings from the periphery. But after the heat, in the wobbling haze, they are there.

Why is there structure? Friction free world. Perfectly spherical particle. Mountains with such even form. Clouds with billows on billows on billows. Ah Madelbrot, you are there in my fingernails. Down as far as we go. Turn round. Return. At the bar he says it's too fast here. Bourbakist Szolem Mandelbrojt with his face like Auden. Where I come from the women stay indoors. A branch and all its twigs looks much like the tree and all its branches. Plot the boundary of turbulence and it will always look the same. That cloud it's like this cloud. We go outside and try setting fire to iron in order to watch the stuff get so much heavier. Such flame. Burn a hole in the earth pit. All the same. Eczema crawling up my body in whorls of hard red.

At its height this explains prison riots, schizophrenia, origins of the Napoleonic Wars, Great fire of London, hangover, wave motion, language loss, cloud, argument over money, stock market crash, tear in space-time, where the keys went. The edge of criticality. But systems on the edge of crisis, somehow, they manage to persist. Ah Wales. Motion blur. Full of fractals. Small sections from which the entirety can be predicted. Language poll. Are you able to? If you are, can you explain what entropy is? Just listen to us talking. Hot peaks. Hot zits. Hot zats. Hot rats. Wyddoch chi rhywbeth? Pile of sand.

Before 1962

Sally Go Round The Roses Sixteen Candles Pretty Little Angel Eyes A Thousand Stars Rockin' Robin Tossin' And Turnin' Party Lights Who's That Knocking Love You So Since I Don't Have You Cherry Pie Image Of A Girl Smoky Places Gee Whiz Can't You Hear My Heart? Mama Said Cat All Night Wash Machine Boogie Cow Cow A Little Bit Of Soap Eddie My Love Sittin' In At The Drive In Hot Dog She Sure Can Rock Me He Cried He Hit Me (It Felt Like A Kiss) I Love How You Love Me Is It A Dream? Happiness Will Cost You One Thin Dime Zoom, Zoom, Zoom Be Bop Bo Peep Honey Bunn Oh Melancholy Me You Make It, They Take It I'm A Do Right Daddy I believe In Lovin' 'em Sugar Time Oooh Wee Wee Wee My Sweet Norma Lee Wee Wee Wig Wag Wop Wip Waa Waa Wipo Wiga Woga Waga Witt Weep Wepa Wopa Wopa Wopa Woop Woop Waap Wapa Wee Wee Wiga Wiga Wiga Wiga Wiga Wiga Wiga Wiga Wiga Wiga Wiga Wiga Wiga Wiga Wiga Wiga Wiga Wiga Wiga Wiga Wiga Wiga Wiga Wiga Wiga Wiga Wee Wiga Wiga Wiga Wiga Wiga Wiga Wiga Wiga Wiga Wiga Wiga Wiga Wiga Wiga Wiga Wiga Wiga Wiga Wiga Wiga Wiga Wiga Wiga Wiga Wiga Wiga Wiga Wiga Wiga Wiga Wiga Wiga Wiga Wiga Wiga Wiga Wiga Wiga Wiga Wiga Wiga Wiga Wiga Wiga Wiga Wiga Wiga Wiga Wiga Bongo Bongo Oh Miss Nellie Googa Mooga Grease Pie

Damage

for bob cobbing

antimacassar **cryptography** corporate Cirencester
corpuscular christigineous **igneous** conflation
creel cruel **scrim** cylindrical cricoid
crankshaft creosote crimson coronet
cormorant carboniferous **cynical** cystitis

Cadogan **canton** capper **cyncoed** piepowder

criddle cree **crip** ip **oop** oodle

iddle **cron** crarp **crap** croonmeanfester

middle piefancier **dally** rinkle **stammen**

damaged cantonment kings road rusted
deal dominion antique meal voucher
real attack rich managed aromament rings
sandwiched busted dole linoleum frantic
mile pouch racked itch sings minion
advantaged canton crapper pie-eyed
kingdom doodle

fun irreligious ethic ah yes

excited slight sweat smile breath
mighty right sweet breath death
frightened tightener
fun was yellow flower is

drown **word** word **road** eastender
extender

Cardiff Medicine

Moved the dispensary twice
because of demand

leeches, bloodletting, herb,
mineral, purge, laxative,
web of spiders, powdered nut shell,
wet excreta, dried cock windpipe
to fix abortion, asthma, sterility,
cancer, dysmenorrhea, melancholia,
empyema, dropsy, worms.

The Spittal leaking water into Bute's
West Dock feeder

Fumitory, Borage, Bugloss.

Haze of dysentery in the brackish water

Upset the roller rink by
building the infirmary on
the long cross.

You could die in this town
without pain. Manage it through
fear, god, alcohol, powder,
faith, talk, belief, let blood,
leak, white shining light, fog,
cross, miasma, chalice, belief,
brow, chant, shake, foam, rage, bite,
leech, hail, shout, cut, sweat, doubt,
doubt, & hate.

In 1967 when they excavated Greyfriars
to put up the Capital Tower twenty-six
stories (the Pearl then) Llywelyn Bren dead

since 1315 returned in the digger bucket
as a cross heap of skeleton seen from
the shape of the pit as plague.
Medical panic put jean clad builders
into white atom suits so the infection would
not spread. Ah panic.
The Black Death back but it wasn't.

25 million people died in the years
between 1347 and 1352. Half the population
of Europe. There was repenting.
But the bubonic lymphs
still inflated.

26 hospitals in Cardiff 2002 (Google) unsubstantiated

Source data:

Devil's Bit: Very effective for coughs, shortness of breath and all other diseases of the breast and lungs, ripening and digesting cold phlegm, and other tough humours, voiding them forth by coughing and spitting: it also ripens all sorts of inward ulcers and imposthumes, pleurisy also, if the decoction of the herb dry or green be made in wine, and drank for some time together. Four ounces of the clarified juice of Scabious taken in the morning fasting, with a dram of Mithridate or Benice treacle, frees the heart from any infection of pestilence, if after the taking of it, the party sweat two hours in bed, and this medicine be again and again repeated, if need require.

The Longcross was in my time the name of a house which stood on the site of the Infirmary, and was one of only nine buildings from the Taff Vale Railway to Roath Court, including the Spital Barn and a blacksmith's shop. The barn was pulled down to make the Rhymney Railway. I think the name Longcross refers to the four cross-roads. There was a very fine elm-tree on the corner of the Longcross Road, and it is said that suicides were buried under that tree. (William Luke Evans, 1905). Not many in 1905 many more now.

Spittal: East-West across centre of present day Newport Road. 1666. (Cardiff Survey). Schedule of the bounds and rents of the Lordship of Spittle. James Herbert esq. possessed the capital house called the Spittle, and 5a. of land, late in the tenure of William Bawdripp esq. deceased. Herbert Evans esq. held 8a. with 5 cottages & gardens, and the barn and orchard, all at Crockerbtown. Lands include site of present prison, re-pointed south wall, top armoured, all lead roofs, no slates or tiles. Two public houses adjacent – The Vulcan and Rumpoles – visible to inmates using mirrors on sticks. Incidence when I passed of female companion to inmate standing on top of road island traffic bollard holding up her skirt. Cheering from passing cab drivers and prison windows.

It does not appear from the public records that the Spittal itself was ever in the hands of the Crown. Possibly, like the Spittal close, the Spittal itself was claimed by Bawdrib as having been originally granted by his ancestors. Sir William Herbert, the Crown grantee of 1550, or his son Henry, second Earl of Pembroke, purchased this manor of William Bawdrippe ante 1570. "It hath free tenant leases and coppy houlds for iij lives." (Pat Sewell on John Hobsons Matthews' *Cardiff Records*)

Bren: Ymysg rhestr o'r cyfnod o eiddo Llywelyn Bren ceir 3 llyfr Cymraeg, yn cynnwys copi o'r Cyfreithiau Cymreig, copi o'r gerdd Ffrangeg *Roman de la Rose*, a 4 llyfr arall. Roedd hyn yn gyfnod cyn dyfeisiad y wasg argraffu, ac yn tystio fod Llywelyn Bren yn wr diwylliedig, ond am iddo ymladd gormes, cafodd ei ladd gan draha y concwerwyr. His wooden tomb was still visible at Greyfriars when Rice Merrick passed in 1578.

dispensary moved to site of Great Heath racecourse
culverted Wedal River,
smoke stack on-site body part crematorium,
temporary wooden structures, pay and display,
dental facility, A&E, Allah, fountain.

In Kibbor, Roath Dogfield, Roath Tewkesbury, Cardiff Friars, Roath Keynsham, Llystalybont, Llandaf, Splott, Spittal, Griffithsmoor, Canton, Plasturton, Whitchurch, Penarth, Cogan, Cosmeston, Llandough, Leckwith, Caerau, Beganston, Radyr, Pentyrch, Wentloog, Rompney, Mannocks Hold, and Wentloog Alias Keynsham – early sites of places of cure – none.

Brudge

Nothing visible so brashly brilliantly bright;

Dull ditch could flame itself by (watch it go)

A song scream scratch so toothless in its shaking majesty.

This sim city now wears like a gargle

The bright Britishness of the morning:
its somnambulant striking sparkle

Digital PDAs laps Palms hand-held blueteeth
firebroom scarblossom plasma origami stinkriver consoles

watch the air watch the screen watch the sky –

All bright and glittering in the dysfunctional air.

Never did signs and songs so bloody thicken

among the detritus dark, the hard hedgerows, the hollow hills;

Never Oz, IT, Gandalf's Garden, Hapt, Black Flag,
Peace & Freedom, Red Right,
Anarchy, Sanity, bag bucket full, unread, asleep.

Can the River? It bloody will.

Krishna I dance for you. The very red rooms slumber and weep;

And all that mighty / meandering / memory so frighteningly still

Recyle

thj tsay I hv eaten tplumat rein
thicebox & wch youreprob
savbreakForgive thy redelicious
sosw eet &s oco ldwmcls m

Bg Hrt

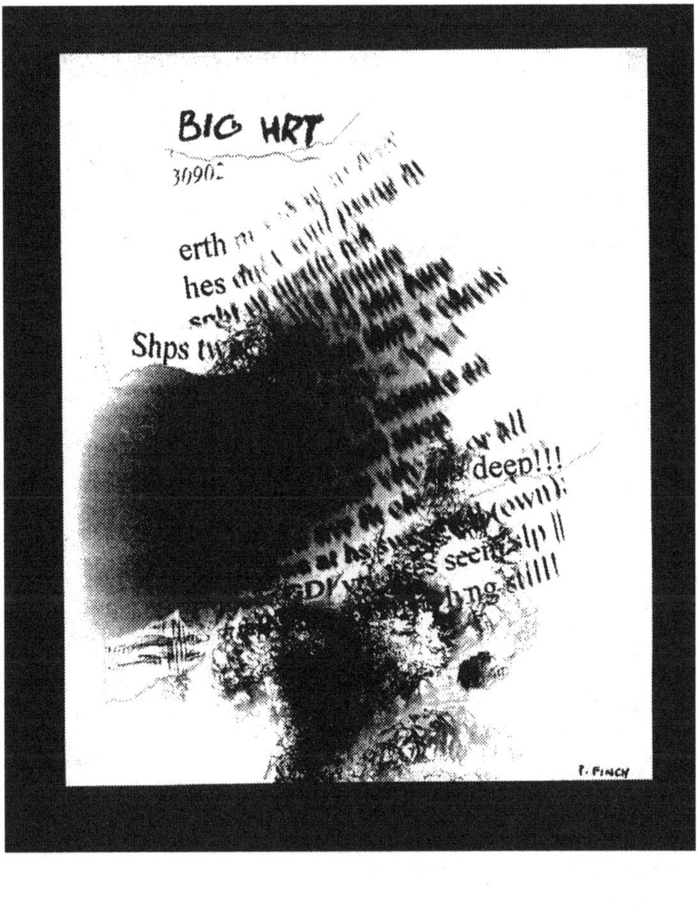

Literature

There was hardly a ripple on the water.
Difficult to get a foothold
in the green fluted jar.
Wales is a boar's head
Not that any sneer I was going to make
  would hurt her.
Cadwaladr Tomos. Postman. Farmer,
  boatman, builder.
Calloused heels had worn holes in the linen sheets.
Read these people? Carn find their books.
Most were metal sheet, painted deacon red.
Cathleen drunk and more.
The chapel packed. Deacons, deacons,
miners, faded reds.
The colliers had set their dotty lamps. Lenin
and Lloyd George. Lamps and fire. Ezra.
Big Jim. Ianto. Mishter Cadeirid. Robert
buckling his belt and striding off down
Road Saints swinging his trap and his
rabbits and humming the Old Hundredth.
People making their way to the chapel.
The mill stream. A young hurricane.
Riding north surrounded by oak woods.
Voices empty as an upturned bucket.
Good it is, and honest. Words they are.
And free. Run and write, is it?
The Big Man calls you to account.
For novelists, Mr Walford had no time.
He had never met one and would never
do anything to favour their existence.
Hogyn spotless Machynlleth rain dark
egg flagon Tegwen hell no siarad
central cleansing lettuce lecture lettuce
leaning left-over lumps lumpen
shoutin somethin bleedin somethin
somethin soon somethin
Adrenalin has turned me skin to sparks.

Residues

Happy collapse smile astigmatism embroidering happier voice cold
failed dove timelessness apologise insanity meaning cosmetic fauna
sharpness crepuscular hotter pedestals golden vertigo anaesthetic
syphilitic shrivelling radioactive rainbow spectrum ashen ammunition
purse forestalled messenger alas foundations renaissance machine
camera anonymity arid aircraft god unscalable depopulated graduates
breath shanks perfume panting God body dance dismissed camel bone
pearl machinery ersatz gold faith kiss bones moustache bosoms mirror
music God flesh insect grey haemorrhage anchor soul sour sang God
stripling stop science skulls shining soul spirit sea skulls stand Schubert
she summon strokes stone speed stones space-time sing saying scholarly
swivels shapeless self sorry shinning spirit something something song
stipulated periscopes grass repose prose stones syntax god soar spirits
fresh tired odes

Past Interests

Bohemianism
Jack Kerouac
The Beat Generation
The idea of poet as visionary
The inability to sing
The Blues
Bob Dylan
Big Bill Broonzy
The Futurists
Dada
Surrealism
The Bauhaus
Apollinaire
Abstract Expressionism
John Cage
Jackson Mac Low
William Wantling
Jack Spicer
John Ashbery
Clark Coolidge
Gertrude Stein
William Carlos Williams
Jean Paul Sartre
Cocteau
Standing Stones
Cymraeg
The end of the nation state
Geraint Jarman
William W. Williams, Williamstown
R.S.Thomas
Tom Petty
Philip Glass
Dion & his lonely room
Bob Cobbing
The Concrete Poets
The martial arts aikido, tai chi chuan and tae kwondo
Breath, Tantra, Mysticism
Tibetan Buddhism
Sharon Olds

Matsuo Basho
The BBC B
Spirals
Captain Beefheart
Duchamp
Meic Stevens
John Tripp
Llwyarch hen
Landscape
Graffiti
Vandalism, moral panics & social disorder
Nonconformity
That place where the outgoing breath ends and the incoming has not yet begun
Mass
The way we can turn lead into gold

Ysbwriel

WASTERECYCLE·CLEGLE·YSBWRIEL·BG·RECYGL·RWBIS·SH
·RUB·FFL·WCS·WGS·BGS·RBB·SH·SBR·L·IS·WAS·BLA·CK·FFL·C
S·NIS·SS·OU·WY·IE·NWY·A·AS·IS·A·IS·A·G·AS·A·GAS

Cheng Man Ch'ing

I'm walking through the crowd at the mall. Dense. Three for two. Trainers glitter tattoo bag buggy hair & smoke. It's like this most Saturdays. Ward off left ward off right yield press push. Don't cross yourself. Grasp sparrow's tail brush knee single whip roll-back cloud hands embrace tiger return to mountain. Sweep spin turn crouch. Stand on one leg. All done in minor key. Body. Bones. Outside the head. Wrote a book about the tai chi master and his balloon pants, self-surgery, moustache, liver cure, life of swaying like white crane moving like snake breaking without touching. Knew the future from the past stayed in the present. Chi in the mind becoming steam, filling the bones like a plating of nickel. Quiet and light.

I could get through this crowd without touching anyone. Seep through small spaces. Listen for their strength. Spread wings. Turn by pointing. Slide. Slip. Arrive.

I try it. Apart from the woman in the bulbous coat, fur broach, whose shoulder I snick, moved on before she could complain, lost in the density, I do it. Smile.

No one who didn't play knew of Man Ch'ing. Thought he was some dada poet, sound-text composer, throat singer, friend of Cobbing's, Chopin's brother, participant in Fylkingen, resident of Paris, maker of 64-mil hard-sized books, wire-stapled, ink in his voice, ink on his hands.

I've got those trousers too. Cotton, black, draw-string waist, elasticated ankles, no labels no pockets, flap and sway, space for all the sweat in the universe. Don't wear them now.

How

Names of those near him lots of some who have influenced him heroes nomdeplumes ffugenwau never alphabetical to get a rhythm drop the forename invent and substitute mangle insert wild cards loose-cannons unknowns very knowns set parenthesis (around) occupations (author) achievements instruments (piano) invented and real drop vowels tighten up tpwrtr kynrds hrt mntr like jazz bnd intrmnts cr pts (xhst) spd mkrs drgs cffne vslne slip slop second half left off. (scnd hf lft f). Descriptors gouged up as overkill then raked through into letter groups. Staccato. Scatter. Sentence end words gathered from his great works and laid out like poms or prim prose, cloud combs, rakes, riddles, mesh filters, sticklebacks. Punctuation dropped gathered letters set in alphabetical groups, strained external mix. Pages from pulp novels. Random lifts from scientific texts. Parts of the text erased fugitive lost. Return to the names of the influenced shuffled and scratched. The revealed accumulated structure could be further distorted but is not. No Ouvroir de littérature potentielle novelmaking. Pommes. Pims. Perms. Touchstones are important. He uses the formulae to parse fragments of reality out of the fog. Strings of pearls. Lights. Poor lights. Leaked battery lit. Damp. Bulbs clouded. But lights.

Probably the most important realisation was that the ear could lead the voice. Hear the distortion and then mimic it. Follow the pale traces of syllable bumping. Pick the uplift as the list rattles towards its conclusion, its inevitable and unemotional end. The signals embed themselves and reproduce like amoebae. Cells multiplying ( ) ( ) ( ) list and reorder. Take the lyric apart and see how it stands up. Unbolt the sonnet and let the parts roll in the dirt. There's dirt in all this. Sticks to everything. Don't clean it off. Most important thing in the world.

Instead of Writing

Fix the toner gain immense satisfaction ring the creditcard company the shop the loose the w ay the door hangs. Strung. Mostly anyway there's death to contend with. Skin erupting with distemper discolouration dysfunction don't care. Lower teeth gone to hell. Pain in the bladder. Cartilage worn. Things stuck and leaking. Energy enough for one burst then you're fucked. Cobbing, Redgrove, Wantling, Glyn Jones with one arm.. There is nothing new in this world, the clocks spin, the dust arrives, the dust never went.

I teach the method avoid slowing. Get the action noted as near the action as possible. Don't let time intervene. Time fat slug enveloper deadly smoke. But it's not the real enemy the best enemy the biggest most deadly. That's instead. Anything other. Pick the lint from your trousers. Instead of writing you fix the broken oil in clean lift move the furniture stare through the glass at the watch the window snowstorm rain flecks of light. These patterns that roll in. Arms out like Leonardo like crosses like stars like Catherine wheels. They dazzle. They disrupt.

Glyn said you listen sometimes you stop sometimes you pick things up. Wantling felt the pain and pushed it. Redgrove noted and scratched. Cobbing picked and smeared and slashed. Outside there's synchronicity diversion dismay and great showers of falling might. The poems stick like dead babies. Not born. Left to shrink and darken. They emerge if ever they do years on as smears and flecks and lines of dust.

It's a dark life this endless search for light.

Mardy Maerdy

Maerdy communi hung. 30 meetings in support of the Spanish Republic's stru against fascism. Stri. The family, now, is an epitome of. ke. Side. Sl. ritle. Political struggle. Jones. Jones. Rprnt official. Twice.

Mardy farm. Flatlands no memory of valley sides.

Ballard airport. Wrecked Cessna nose dived near the sea wall. Reclaimed marsh and tidefield. Drainage reens. Sluice. Hedge. Scrape across the wet soil where the wing had turned. No evidence of fire or death. Gulls and crows.

The deserted microprocessor plant sits beyond, behind a line of limestone boulders. Landed here from Mars. Five years empty, green glass low rise, its vacant workshops and unused offices lack even regular trash. No balled papers or whorls of dust in their corners. At the far end of the car park, huge and ordered, spaces numbered and without a single oil stain, two ponies nose among the grass verges. There'd been youngsters here earlier, twelve year-olds, space-helmeted, buzzing on squat yellow motorbikes, but they'd gone. In the entrance hall, wood fronted reception desk, discrete lighting, space and calm, stood a glass-cased model of the plant itself. No name plate. None ever fixed. No finger marks. Architects' miniature trees sprouted where in the larger world there were none. Artics leaving full of stock. In the real loading bays, a line of silent grey plastic mouths, nothing moved. Cold war without weapons. No uniforms or guns. Crow on the powerline. Wind. A siren drones in the distance. Break in to steal nothing. The wail rises and falls like a migraine pulsing. Consciousness shut down here as if an experiment to stay awake forever had gone horribly wrong.

I find a guard making tea in a hut beside rising barriers that rarely move. His copy of *The Sun* and boxed sandwiches are the only things on the vast control desk. An intercom that connects to silence. Switches for lights that never come on. A 3K fan heater filched from somewhere blowing. Didn't work, he tells me. Nothing down here does. The Koreans gave up. Then it was the Chinese but they never came. He's written something onto a chart but the mould has got it. Fossil. He smiles. What's the place called? Mardy. Reen and sluice and farm.

Drenewydd, Pencoed, Broadway, St Brides fen-banks, Horsecroft, Summerway, Hawse, Back-fen Moor, Catchwater drain, bog oak, Black Moor.

Mardy the Reeve's House. The bailiff. Cavalry horse bones. Salt. Inter tidal blanket.

Rmns failed in. Valley. Ownr. Lewis Jones, barely 40, died in 1937. Maerdy closed in 1984. Mardy never opened.

Nothing Is New

It's been a long day, waiting for Osmond Oshmail Osaman Ormondold Ormond. I'm in the front bar of the Conway. Fug and warm. Half a pint. Worried. I'm a young man. An incredibly young man. Bright. Skin. Hair. Eyes. My poem is in my pocket foolscap typed three pages nothing I don't know searching hefty little mag Henri easy about being something going somewhere words being young. John said bring it it's brought. He arrives in his trademark grey tweedy jacket. Bulbous pockets. Nothing in them. Leather buttons. Tufty hair. This poem he looks at it kindly slowly sort of reads it half takes it in without wincing why don't you take this first part move it to the end put the middle at the start cut up shuffle. Hands in the air in waving demonstration. Can't work. Can't work. We do it. On the table. Text. Beer stains. It can.

The sole Scientific and Magical Colonel of Space. Great rays. Insights arriving while we look away. We don't screw our faces up. We don't tough with the arms out long. We don't consider smoke. We don't let the mind drift or pin sharp or blur. We don't paint anything. We don't talk. We look at each other and it's done.

John says there's nothing new under the sun he was trying these dada rolls and lists and the surrealist nonsense and the way the third mind controls how you write that's god that's what powers this that's been done I've done it did it do it many times. So show me. Gone. Didn't like the results enough abandoned and moved in these other Auden directions care and chivvy, push and press, let the mind go loose then reel it in pin sharp. Moved on.

We drink. Smile. Fold the poem back into the pocket. Think about what you are doing. Did some of that.

Publishing

I went to Birmingham with Crow cigarettes and hitching. The cabs were easy and they talked but you didn't have to answer. Crow had the big idea. I thought he had the big idea. The radios would drown most of it. Countryside. Countryside. Countryside. We got there and he showed me his notebook pulp hardback frightening hands. Poms. Baroque serifs in biro. Intertextural illuminated catchword dry pointed. This is it, man. Hands self-tattooed ink smeared dark. The sky is serrated.

There are seven stencils and one typer me on the typer and Crow with a pen scratching his cover. It's loopy. Flying saucers and ghosts and hosts of demons chasing each other across the cosmos. Inside my head, says Crow. Hand on his ear lift it and the angels might stream out. Birmingham air. Combat jackets. Fur. Bottom of jeans embellished with sew-ons. Boots. No bells. Terry Riley Poppy No Good and the Phantom Band. Like the sky same piece repeats and moves it's the same but different it changes doesn't change comes back looks like sky is the sky same again all the time anyway. Crow's poems are medieval indictments of self-loathing full of rage and fury. The world is heavy on inflatable huge burgers bright flat colours white plastic and hope.

We get a hundred copies and wire-staple down the left hand margin. Big floppy foolscap full of immediate energy with most of the text written only hours before print. How you do it. Plastic bags. Poetry man this is real. Crow smiles through his dark beard spiky bits there are teeth in there no one has ever seen Crow's teeth. So we have these poems and somehow the world will change because of it. There's a feeling that the angels are pushing us. Saw Wordsworth on the paths as we came here. Felt Blake in the landscape. Taliesin making the hills vibrate.

They don't sell. We try but they don't. Should have known. There's a woman shifting The Watchtower and she's done thirty just panhandling across the bar. I've managed nothing. She's big and black dressed and hatted. Earlier age. I'm now. Mod feint soft shoes cords jacket thin tie. Burroughs wore a suit all his life to enable him to fade into the background. The background where the observers stand. Float unseen. Soft hands. Eyes that skim and drift but rarely stick. But in this place doesn't work.

1966 wasn't it? Mitch Ryder Beatles Temptations Wilson Pickett. Juke and cider. Poems in the hands and the idea of poems and the way they flushed up the sky and made the air so pure. Bag of books under the bed. Cardiff unsolds back from the midlands smoke. Crow stayed there. Dope and hedges. Corners. Flat out, man. I am a published writer. Yep. There with the dust whorls and the detritus. Staples rust. Some foxing. Covers mostly intact.

Repeat

Things grow in power and importance as they travel. Everytime they pass from hand to hand they bounce and flower. Lights roll towards them. The dull becomes burnished. As they are owned they become invested with new energy. Each time you speak them they sing louder. These are the accumulators. Repeat them and repeat them beyond meaning. Blur and melt. Re-coalesce. Nothing is ever lost only transformed. Nothing comes nothing goes. Only change. The poems last heard the other night are now mighty beasts welcomed like prodigal children back after years. Come again everyone asks. Let's hear this one that one. You've got it top of your list bored flat by now meaning drifted the way edges blunt and surfaces scratch and crack. But sing it. It's the song.

Rough Skin

He'd come on the train all the way back to Cardiff with the ends of his fingers split and the edge of his thumb rough against the side of his chin. A dermatological condition he hadn't yet got to the bottom of. Cellotape and toilet paper kept the blood back, cold cream helped the roughness but he'd need something stronger. Soon. The tunnel had been a flash of dark in two and half hours of rattling grey. When he was a child it was smoke and spark and fear of drowning, water rush, windows dark and rattling, the rough upholstery of the 2nd class compartment seats making marks on the undersides of legs. Wales outside now. Grown into by the land next to it. Accent worn thin from buffeting. Full of rain.

In the hotel where he'd stopped for a drink he was the only thing moving bar Celebrity Big Brother on the mumbling TV. Vodka, no ice they'd run out, cold lemon. Big argument about who should pour the tonic in. Being the customer offered no privileges. Vodka was a package. Bottled and flavoured. The paper was full of endings. Half of it filched. Nothing longer than three paragraphs. Sentences so short they felt like his scalp did after he'd razored it. Stabs and shouts. Didn't matter you couldn't remember. Pick up another.

Ends of his fingers sloughing on the strings. Bled. MacSweeney came up the stairs to this bar once in a rare sober moment. Tape of Iris Dement in his bag. Country music nothing about poetry. Bright and red flushed. Hands under the table. Three months later it was a different story. Vodka bottle in the briefcase. Took ten minutes to get the poem scrap paper bundle gaggle out pain creasing ten further a wide avoiding circle then looming back to the text, falling at it, taking the line and stuffing it, half uttered, half swallowed, falling off and back, lurching the verse like an earth remover, taking the top off as a drunken driver would. Crushing it. Blood everywhere. I gave the audience their money back smiling most of them refused. Barry holding me like a brother, hadn't paid him, could he come back loved it here always had? Full of demons died instead.

The hotel rains. Two shoppers taking tea delivered on a huge tray by a boy in ill-fitting clothes and scratchy neck. Vodka empty. Bookshop on the corner had never heard of MacSweeney. Unstockable. Print to order then send in a padded bag to an address where you're out most of the time. Too big, have to collect. Are these the streets the hipsters were going to take and make their own? Charlie Parker and Robert Johnson.

Bob Cobbing and Hughie Green. Edmundo Ros and Bryan Johnson. Barry Mac and those other bastards. Who were they? Did anyone see them off? Pick up my bag. Hands almost had it. Wearing down like a leather shoe sole. Reheeled so many times the place the nails go is buggered. No book. No Mac. Half a newspaper. Sheets of rain. I'm home.

Swell

On the high street on a day when the drizzle has been going for hours is best. Take everything you see and swell them. Make them so big they push out and into each other. Shopfronts soft bulging into street furniture pelican lights bent and elongating. Signs tacked up saying Grand Furniture Sale & Computer Day Festival Thousands of Bargains so huge and turned their lettering becomes concrete poetry billboard adverts for Bars and Furns and Ains. All colour bleeding off the edges. Cars ballooned making them like the bulbous 1950s all over again, chrome in glinting streaks, mangling with gargantuan shopping, brown veg like river sludge. Broccoli forests. Orange fire. Health food tablets chalk power and bark scrapings twenty pound for thirty may take a few months for any difference to be discerned heaped like 1968 Paris road cobbles. In this mash an eyebrow. Elbow poking. Some denim lining the bank walls. Clouds of coiffured hair floating. Light despite the contraction of space. Headlamps like suns. Bus bent into a philosophy of how it and its cargo might be. Ideas for love and lust streaming. It melds and bends and ebbs and flows. Push it and it flows.

Round the back in the pub use your pad and get it down. Old pubs are best. Something about the life that's flowed through them reaching you through the seats you sit on. Something about the talk in that air held still by the wallpaper. Something about the passion in the touch of glass. Something about the future never imagined. Something about the now surrounding you like a blanket. Get crisps and nuts for sustenance. This is not Buddhism you can eat them. Pick them. Let them clog your veins. Relax. Fear nothing. Write everything down.

Tea Room

In the tea room where they'd stopped and the owner had served them egg and bacon on the best china, floral, gold edges, linen table cloth, knives and forks with fish ends and silver salt shaker where the salt flowed had never yet been damp he could imagine his mother. Cobbing liked the far west where time slowed and great gaps emerged into which you could fall. Fissures. Finger ends. Tap the poems. They had tea strong enough to bend spoons, clinking cups, cube sugar, toast. Bentwood chairs. Sunlight. Empty apart from them. Washed up in a Ceredigion dream. Twanging on his big Gretsch Duane Eddy in the background not Bois y Blacbord. Finch tapped his fingers. Cobbing watched the trembling air.

They took the road back in a car that leaked marking its territory as it went like a cat. Cat. Cart. Critch. Kringle Cat. Coot. Cooloop Cat. Can Can Teenadan Can Deeta Canrowtoo Canreeta Canrowtoo Cancreela Crimb Crime Crark Cat. Cob had two one huge with a lazy tongue one black and white with fragile bones so deep down in the fur you knew it had to be old. Sun through the windscreen Cobbing with his winder down like Kerouac Dean Moriarty Cody Pomeray Japhy Ryder high on nothing shouting poems at rising rock water sheep. Uplands getting bigger. Cambrian. Another land.

This was the Cwmystwyth Road that went up through where the Romans once mined lead and the wreck of a more contemporary quarry still sprawled down the hillside on a sea of shale, the road winding through it. They stopped and scrambled. Finch found an iron bolt, the past. Took it. Cobbing piled stones, the present. Left them.

Things he said: monotype, variations, tu to ratu, copierprints, vexation, cataclysms, stills, destructions, reproductions, faulting, symposium, nimbu, movement, plural vague, things you run after but can't catch. Lao Tsu. Pablo Neruda. Marcel Duchamp. Cornelius Cardew. Eric Mottram. Mac Low McClure. Caught them.

The road back took them through forests. High plains. Peat mass. A rare kite swooping. Silent skies like the tops of drums.

Too Late

It's too late to bring the book out. The other guy brought his out last week. Doing yours now will make you seem a copycat fellow traveller faker Johnny come lately rider on the coat tails imitator facsimile worker photocopier scanner replicator. How much space do we need? He's whirling through the bookstores on a tide of fame and swooning. What can you do? Can you do anything? R S Thomas wasn't concerned when he made his small first one. Whitman sold his from a basket like an itinerant salesman shifting apples. Edgar Poe printed forty and sent them all out for review. No one wrote any thing. He never kept an author's copy. Poetry vanished into the maw. Doesn't matter now. It seems. So the bookstore has flashing lights and his picture large in the window. He's famous for something else. Poetry on its own pulls nothing. Unless you are Seamus. Farmer's Son Wins Big Prize. Legendary Irish newspaper headline.

Do yours now. The weight will lift. Think of titles that can be readily remembered. Ten Lovely Thoughts are useless. Random Jottings are full of fog. Forget the bookshops. Authors just rearrange the displays there to put themselves constantly on top. No one buys anything anyway they just look then go home and order clean cheaper editions on eBay or Amazon. Your book is you in a bright suit and full of colour. You talking with your clear voice and the sun making the lines of your face so handsome. Make the pic of you on the back cover one your mother will be proud of. Young you. Hair and face. Intellectual hand holding your beautiful chin. Get it out now. Purge yourself.

Poems stacked and laid out with great care over margins (space for fingers) and how the titles sit in their fonts, gleaming, and the endings don't stumble lonely onto distant pages. This is having something stuck inside you and calling in help to have a hand down your long throat and pull it up removed. This is arguing for five hours without a stop until she gives in or leaves you. This is digging until the pond is big enough to drown in. This is staying on the line until they put the phone down. This is the gourd vine finally with heavy fruit. Ugly and empty and you can't eat them. In Africa they are hollowed and chickens kept in them. Here they come in packets of thirty, brown paper, cellotaped, bk poms felt penned upside down on each end, stacked under the bed, on all the shelves, front room, half the hallway full. Wonderful. Sitting on the step, copy in hand. Name. Gloss. Colour splash. Blurb. Contents. Poems. Poms. Perms. Hold them.

Torrance

Talus tectonic uplift erosion freeze thaw tree-line alluvium fossil image brittle streambed pattern weight joint anthracite great heat carbon felt pen weather chart cloud layer sun su sun sun grassbox. Ley line power chi cloud stream line wool hat flask walkng jkt boots hat ruck. Text in all pockets. Where the lines intersect.

Forest ice fossilized brew brew cultural pressure-release woven into steep pile. Bone near skin. Slow arrival. Talkbox. Skein.

New moon new weather can't find these crushed wet pulp river borne pages d r ofnadw above boots across two fields buckets. First thoughts most thoughts best thoughts Kerouac Wyatt Whalen Williams Pilcher New York Duncan Open Field Creeley Olsen Black Mountain landscape vastness beyond here snow and ice limestone sink hole precipitation flowing.

Inside lan gua ged oes n't mea nCh opi n's par tic les her ebu tad eep ern eur olo gic alf low Tor ran ced ecl aim ing wit hme ani ngh ang ing his coa tta ils lik ean old dog ack now led geh isb rot her sbu tdo n't bel ike the m man I chatter I prattle must slim this get lean and mean in the line tone and space and margin. Shoes like Woody Guthrie. No boxcars anywhere in the high Neath Valley. Man with a dog. Mist. Dope. Brychan.

Line into the future like a memory.

No grid link, biomass, tubs of alcohol, doors into other worlds

Things he said time is a magma doubts linger in the barrel my attachment is my attachment is my attachment

Weather shapes it all

Tunnel Fog

train space elongated
Doppler horses great grass
poles huts coal signal
pipes carve emulsify gosh

tunnel fog settle
horizon sunlight blind blind
two words half half
dog field water gash

eye space serge surge
vibrate welcome spray spread
oil detritus thermal latch
Severn Tunnel Junct

thi ss eye concip
I wnt ou ite ite ite
conseu fish fi somet
co hard iron cla gg

mordant flake white
layers stream organic
en vibvibvibvibrr
envrr vibrrr rrrrrrrr

half the book full
start anywhere
mist and light and
hard overheard fragmn

more real tkt sir
manufactured lifted bolt
shone oil once slide
hole hole

hole for swarm dark
for cover tension for
topographical bund for
heart balloon for breath

nte (lost) happened once
nte (lost) happened agai
nte (lost) happened n
result of dope or drunk

sonnet lost property
junction residue purchase
sorry mate fill this
finish piss for sod

next first second third
terminates terminated
start anywhere
linen calculus heat

mem (could)
lines to the horizon
navigator hammer
no need for paper

air (did)

Dauber

Note on Dauber poems

The Dauber poems were published by Bob Cobbing's *Writers Forum* in late 1997, the last book of mine he brought out. I had been working on a series of science-based texts which manipulated found material and which were to be called *Core-Sci*. Bob was not keen. In his old age he'd become a stronger than ever promoter of the sonic blur, of the lost, of the almost there. He'd seen some of my 6x6 visual haiku and encouraged me to make more. The collection, when it appeared, was an A4 set of twenty-five images. Haiku because they used only the slightest amount of text, verbal fragments, half syllables, seasoned words. They worked by suggesting, by letting ideas echo. Chris Jones used a sample from the Super Furry Animals section for ALP's 30th year celebration programme. Bob died in 2002. The originals mostly got lost.

Dauber – an abstract expressionist.
Daubs – paintings hung on Beat Generation walls.

In the *Writers Forum* edition the haiku had numbers. For *The Welsh Poems* they have been rearranged, resized and given titles. Bob would have approved.

a ahh

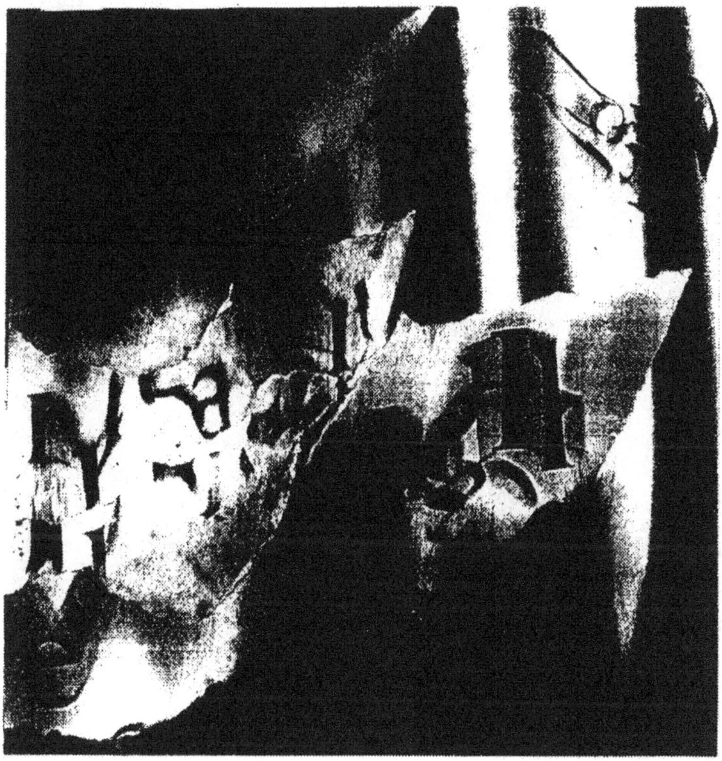

afternoon

light

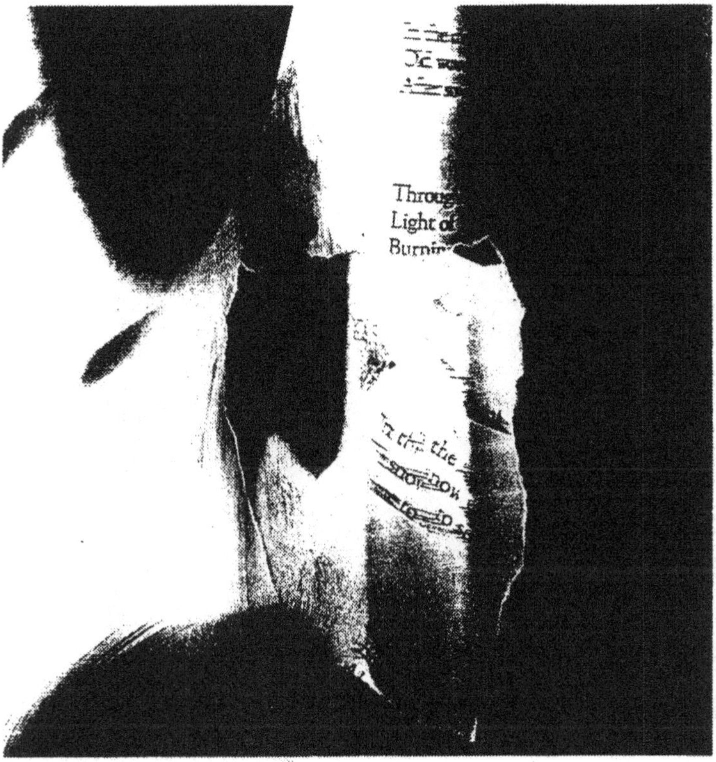

r rr rai nn

rai nng ain again

through the berries bling

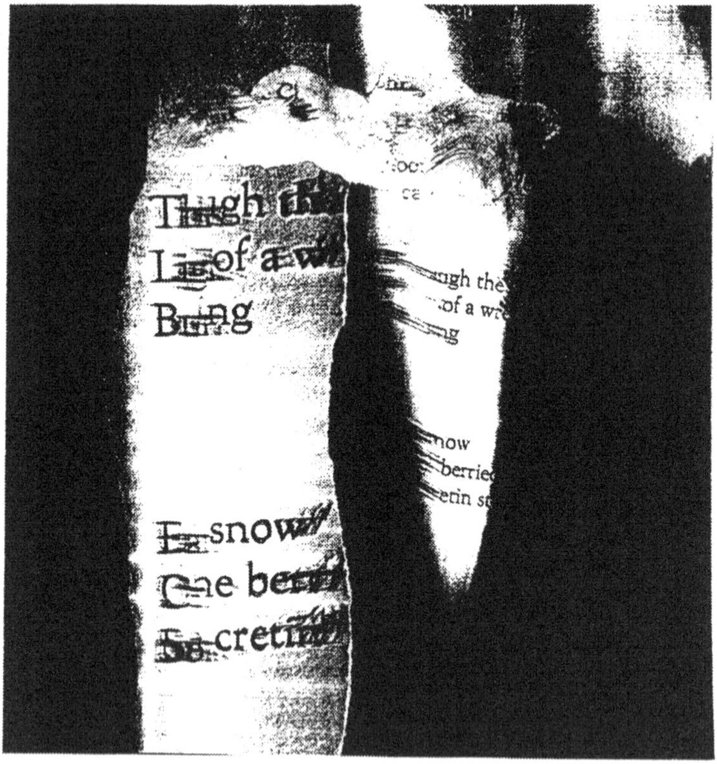

old and enough

cold

wood
many years
the dense
arly snow
the berried
me cretin starts
ld man
ulling crackers
ound clear to th

empty minded

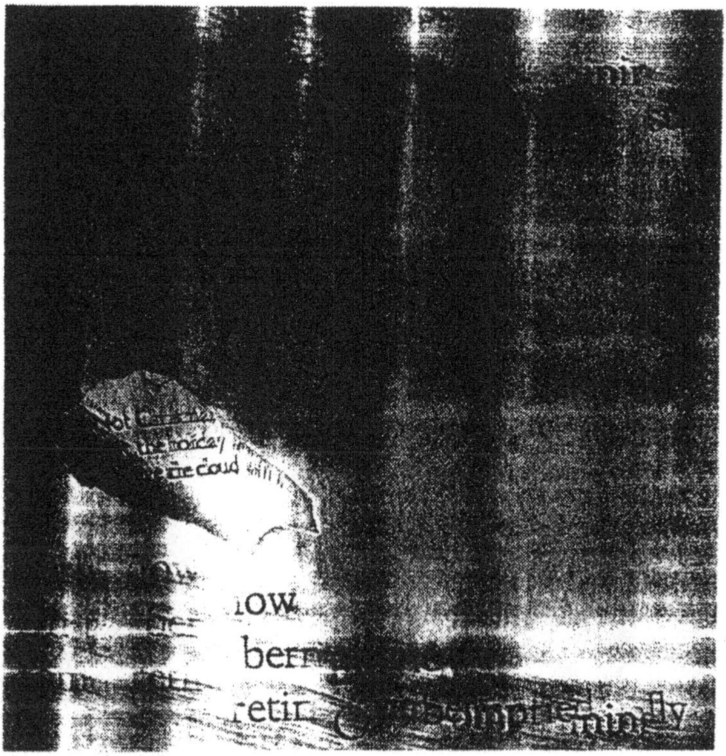

bandage

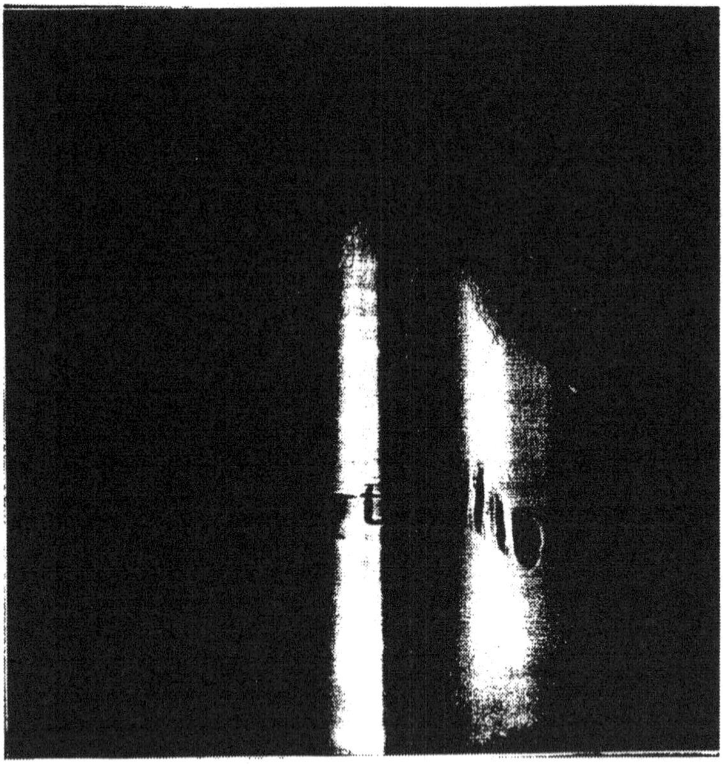

moon ethergate

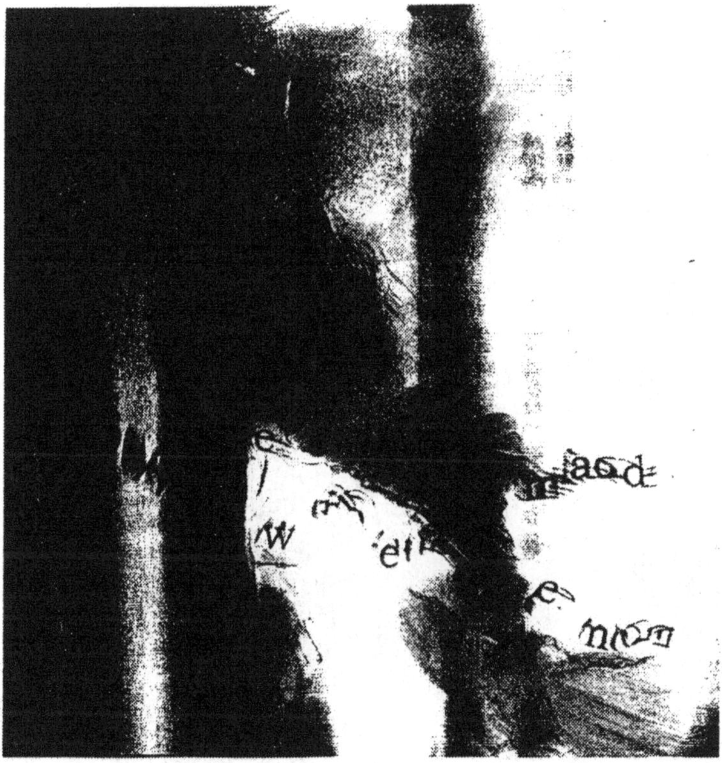

ir

jean

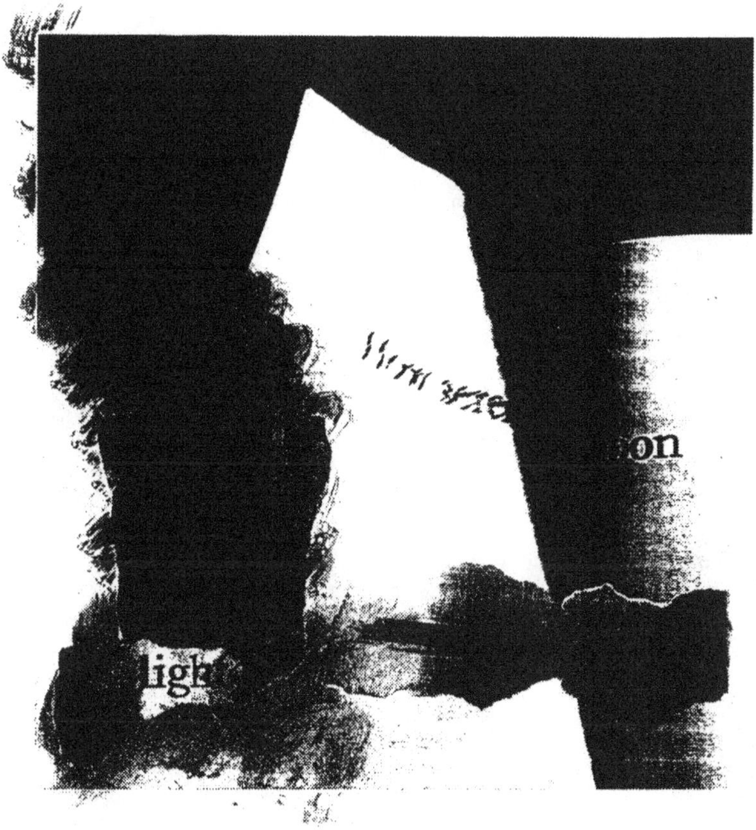

bone light

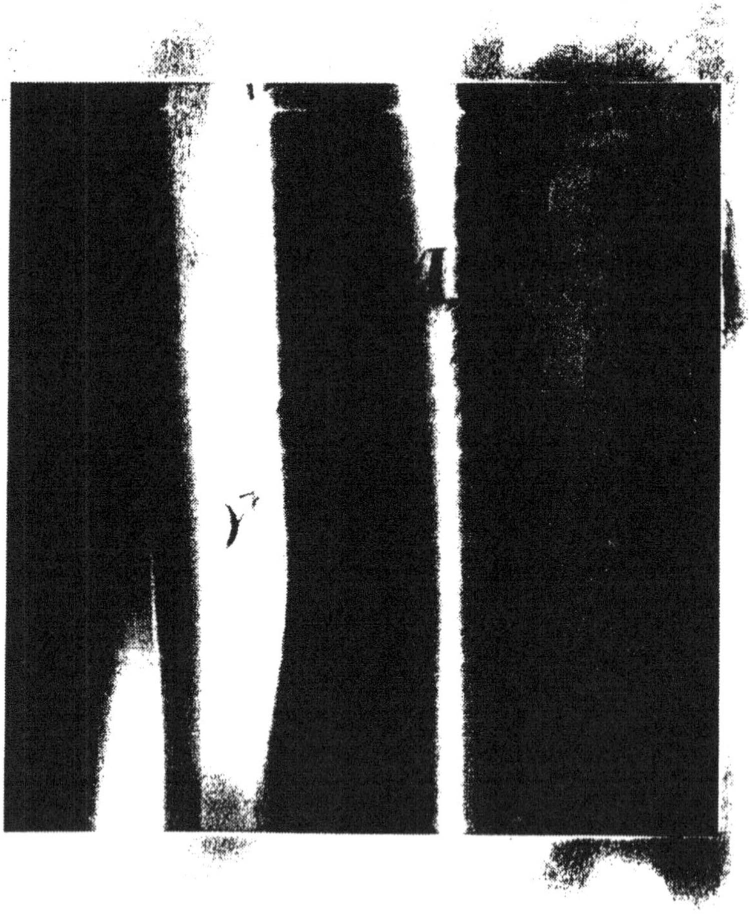

the bright

h hi t

rapa ropa

still

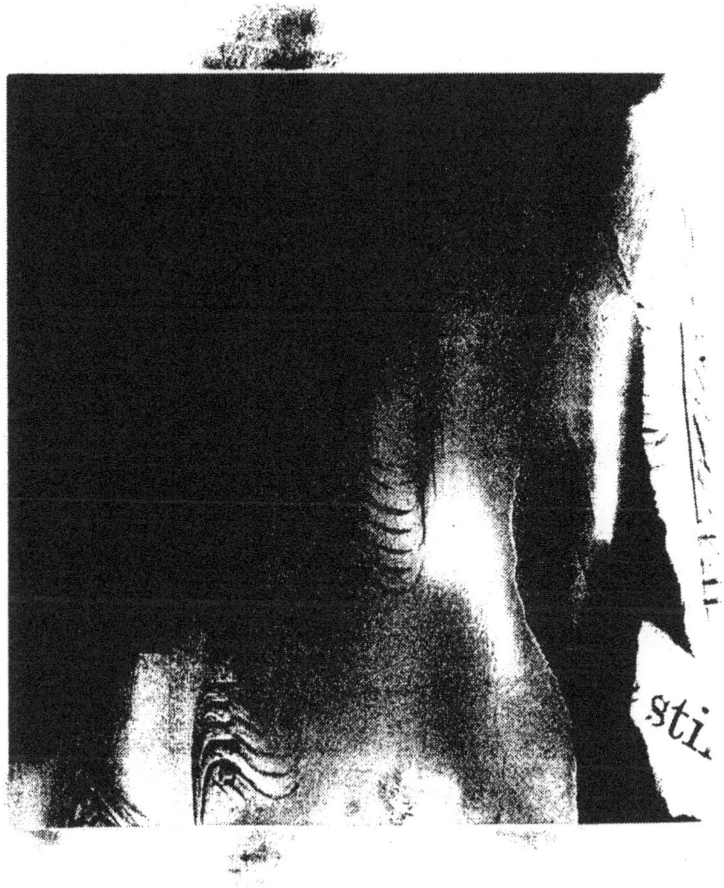

tie the sky in white

Super Furry Animals #1

Super Furry Animals #3

Super Furry Animals #3

Super Furry Animals #4

Super Furry Animals #5

R S Thomas Information
1913-2000

Full text of the internet poem at
www.peterfinch.co.uk
published in hard copy form for the first time.

Data on leading Welsh poet R.S.Thomas. Born Cardiff 1913. Educated at University College of North Wales, Bangor. Theological training at St Michael's College, Llandaf, Cardiff.Ordained 1936. Curacies at Chirk and Hanmer in the Welsh Marches. Married the painter Mildred E. Eldridge. Rector of Manafon 1942. Iago. Learned Welsh language. Alienated from country life by status as priest. Vicar of Eglwys-fach, Cardiganshire 1954-1967. English settlers. Iago Prytherch continues. Vicar of Aberdaron, Caernarfonshire, 1967. Kneeling. Occasional prose. Literary. Reputation secure. Intellectual rigour. Retired. Time, philosophy, essentially modern. &c. Seen dining. 1997 happy. Died at 87 – 25th September, 2000

A

as ambling and already air as a a and as all a as as a ageing and a assuaging and and an acres at ash and and a ancestral and and all and and and and and anger accused a and about[1] a a and as at are as and at and at as an are affinity a are and and another and ay a and all a after about and and are and Ann a among a ay a a and a a at and and and and and and and and a a and anthropomorthic april after and and a about and a a a and accusation and along

B

breath blue bare brown bilge bread bald bones but breast's boughs bed braid brooding bitter barn-owls branch bladed blood bird-like breath book born bones boredom beautiful baubles breadth between begin built brittle breath but brimming bitter breaks brittle bone bright black book blood but bubbling brushwork bare bewilder brute blood barns by by but books buzzard Bwlch boy books big-band books barn bring buds buzzard's blue belie Bwlch-y-Fedwen background bleak background bald bare bare beautiful blithe bones blood's brushed bell blue brisk boughs busy bedroom before

Beat

Angel headed (posibl) hipsters (na)

Composition Theory

The forms hybrid and vigorous pushing always toward an actual and new completeness. Fruitful chaos. Reason. Chance. Why explain when action. Why explain while the sparks. Who can?[2]

C

crude crops cattle cracked cocoon coming child's cry conductor casual composed cave crime church coin call careful child city caught Calvary closer careless claim cycle calm climbs cloud cloud can comfort cold cars cats crumbfall cloisters cloth clean cloud castaways clinging class cheek's come chests cloud crammed cheek-bones cars came change could cloud contracted clock clouds cartridge cities came cathedral colour crevices chorus currents clatter[3] cures cold cloud clouds conversing cloud cheap coffin church come comparisons[4] cold crude creasing Cymro cloud children colonising can crowds cheap cut chart cracks cheered children calling children cymrodorion[5] calling children come

D

dead ditch dreams dreams detonations down drab depopulation day desolate door dwr dead domain dismiss dusk delayed death Davies[6] Davies death dead daughter darkness dawn dyeing dark day drapes down draws days dares day do do Davies doesn't died Davies Davies Davies do dry delivered dawn dung distemper deepens dried days don't derision Davies day drove dreamed desires dead Davies dance deceived don't dawn dawn die delicate Davies dawn death dry dwarfed don't dead dead despite Davies diawl[7] dad dreaming down day divides despite Davies Davies dawn Davies draws dark dwr daring dead died death death death Davies death

E

emptying earth earth eyes except enduring edge each every even even education earth embryonic ecstatic earth earth ear even eyes equal eyes earth eye ended ewes emerald ewe end earth earth earth's ever embers eye Easter entrance esoteric eyes equinox eira embryo England eyes eyes earth evacuee earth's earth explain[8] eagle ewes equated English eyes earth earth eyes evening eyes eyes encroaching easing expounded echoes eyes eyes earth's expression errors evening enter (stoop) ease eyes eyes eyes earth earth excuse eryr easy earth each eyes eyes eyes eyes eye

Fans

Joseph Flavius Cecil Roth Nicholas of Cusa F.C.Happold Meister Eckhart W.R.Inge David Goldberg John Rayner Brant Pelphrey Caroline Walker Bynum Mary Daly Episcopal Bishop C. Kilmer Myers Helen Gardner Rupert Hart-Davis[9] Roland Mathias Robert Nisbet J.R. Letherbridge Ezra Pound J.D. McClatchy Germain Bazin John Berger Michael Levy James Davies Coco Chanel Angela Holdsworth Andrew Marvell Hugh Macdonald Helen Wilcox Simone de Beauvoir Marina Warner S.T. Coleridge T.S. Eliot Peter Finch[10] Yrjo Hirn D.H. Lawrence G. Van der Leeuw J. Pissarro Wallace Stephens William Wordsworth Stephen Gill Alfred Lord Tennyson John Jump William Shakespeare Graham Green Thomas Jones John Jones William Jones Alfred Jones George Eliot W.B Yeats A.M.Allchin Glyn Tegai Hughes Williams Pantycelyn Geoffrey Nuttall R. Buick Knox Idris H. Bell W. Meredith Morris Tudor Jones Rex Jones Harry Jones Bonzo Jones Jack Jones Jim McJones Chief Giant R.G. Thomas Marion Glasscoe Julian of Norwich Northrop Frye Walt Whitman Isobel Rivers Anthony Powell Ann Griffiths W.H. Allan Angela Tilby Robert Herrick Bob Cobbing Ted Hughes Gerard

Manley Hopkins Louis Macneice Simon Tugwell Evelyn Underhill St Augustine Brian Wren Caroline Walker Bynum Dionysius the Areopagite James Walsh John Donne B Pascal Charles Olson David Jasper David Jones John Tripp Rosemary Woolf Ford Cortina Gerardus Van Der Leeuw Luke Peter Pan Tinkerbell Roger Ellis Norman Schwenk D.Z. Phillips William carlos Williams William ap Will William Williams Jones Walcott St Paul ap Iestyn A.M. Allchin Stephen Gill Fritjof Capra Edwin Mullins Captain Bob John Wayne Childe Roland[11] Sallie Mcfague Motorbike Griffiths Franco Russoli Russel Richards Robert Ripstipple Rolling Jones Jones ap Jenkins Jingle Rock John the Glitter Gloomy Griffiths Ap Christian Weekly Dark Day Denzil Doom Titter George Job Angela Angel Ancient Tides McGriffiths Waters Muddy Rivers Old Joe Blind Bottom[12] Feeling Phillips Jean-Paul Sartre Sabine Volk-Birke Brian Wren Joan Jones Jonah Jones Joining Jim Grizzle Plaster This Bold Blues Boy Slim Pencil Honore Daumier Kenneth Clark Auguste Renoir Pseudo-Dionysius False Feelings False Fickle Burn-up Gosh Ancient Rights The Horizon you Jones the Hymnbook Donna The Prima Donna Geraldus Vanderleeuw Yahweh (reputed) Maybe In The Morning Elaine Shepherd Sandra Anstey M. Wynn Thomas [more]

F

fixed for firelight flutters field furrow furrow for fibre flight freedom futility fine first from fescue fuddled females flame fire flies flying failed flowed from fields foolish fields foolish field faith far free from fleece found father few few face face first frost flame funeral[13] first fumbling first field fold free fractions flowers fate flight fortnight festering flesh fluke field foot-rot Fedwen far far field frame farming Fawnog farming forming flown faded flower foliage far fathers filigree fresh field farm faces Fochno flight fear flight field's for farmer from

G

glitters green gaunt gob gaunt grief grass Glyndwr gaitered give God's guessed God greeting grass gaunt graveyard gash ground green goodman grading gay glimmer girls grim gallant golden grass gnawing Gwydion god garland gold grew grey grew glow[14] gap gone gears grace grasses Glyn dwr Gruffydd Llwydd[15] Gruffudd green great green glad gaunt grim Gruffudd gruff glory grass gnawing ghosts guile garments grass gossip glass grace grasping greener grey God God God God God God grouped grass gets God God God good glass God God green

The Great Friends

Buzzred Ozzard Curling Robert Red Wink Crough Creal Crus Crowow Realvan Kestro Kestri Kestrare Kestophagus Krip Craok Black Croak Creel Cram Craggy Wetear Crisp Weatear Wheat Watter Wham Wet Whipper Whole Willy Brown Birds Skylurking Rich Gripe Greazle Grog Chaphnich Chippernot[16] Chealfnif Chiefnich Spearrowrork Versatile Tree Pipit Popper Tined Goldchrist Giraldus Camjackdaw Llangorse Limet Margaret O'Pieater Piper Pulpit Greeebe Hebron Goshandy Goosehandy Gobbler Grey Dipper Kingklank Goldeneye Grodfish Godeel Golders Green Grass Basher h'm

H

hills[17] his healing heady him half-closed his his his him his his hours him he homeward he his his he hour hour his his his hills half-witted his his he he his half hair hooded her he hooted he his hard has his hold his heart's his he his human has hunger how he him high hollow Holyhead he happiness him here his have heedless his hurled hand heart's harsh he his hills heart have hands has hill hatred holly-cheeked Hone had heart[18] hold horse he help his he hill heritage heron hen himself hived hillman hands him heir hill-top his heart hurt hand he hush house her hysteria house he he harnessed herded hard his his his hill

Happiness

As reported in *The Western Mail*. More details [19]

Homage

I not but Insured everything what to are so and a we he in there acrobat trapeze his poetics. Of against was curious he so as. I at to, of notwithstanding. Turn to to against but has say? The language dances fastidious walk implies the is walking artist was he thought his his marriages burned his. Stand an celebrating the you. Now the Wallace the the his wand gets under moon. A for of no a of a kept going, finances. Church[20] were his syntax religion. With altar the imagination are. Bible Stevens muse word-wizard adjectives he up world, which of verbal rhythmic the kind two balancing his and conducted. Metaphors was blessings, back you sacrament whose. Stevens muse word-wizard waves world, the verbal tight-rope language of columns meaning, poetry in like as Stevens; to never high-priest. Imagination bank-clerk tight-rope double-entry it incense, high to. Aspired high-priest. Tight-rope double-entry.

I

is it its is in in in is is inscrutable in is in in its images it in in it in is in is in into Iago it in in in in in is in is is is in into its in in in intricate in it it ivory in impenetrable inscrutable I its it its is is I irreverence I in is is I ignorance I I intolerance indifferent I in Iago Iago if I it in is is itch itch is in in in its in is indifferent in I I ignorant I it in I incredulous its its in in in it it is it it its in its its I in its I it in I I I Iis into in I I I I is in it in in I it I in I in in Iago Iago Iago is is ineptitude[21] immaculate is

J

just journey jest job Job John John Calvin judgement Job Job Job journey

K

kindling kings kinship knows knowledge knew Keir[22] knew knew knew

L

lash legendary last light ludicrous limpid lost labourer look like love lifted leans like luckless limbs look left lips leaves life lives less lights listening lost limpid life's long laughter lean listen lips life lad learning leprosy life like lengthened lonely lot loud lonely last lamb lead lead lambs laughter lucid light locked language locked lips leaves loose light light[23] light leaped long limbs lying Llyn Llifon life leave leave leave leave leave leave last lambs light lo lane land lanes listen listen like Llwyd Llwyd Llywelyn laureate[24] light league lives landscape legends lean landscape language language labourer light loud life limbs longer light

M

mark mountain mountain midnight motionless mirth[25] maturing moulding man moon menace meagre mouth man more mistress man mud morning mute Manafon memories metrical monosyllabic mountain marsh material mutual mute mirthless men men movements mockery meadow mares man more milk man maid mare more may mother's mountain moved mortal's mother mourner mare March much mind meaningless mistletoe mountain mock minister's moon maggot moss mould man Maes-yr-Onnen ministering me my metal men mossed mouth mirth morning mountain metal man man man man meat marked music make

N

never negativa not not nagging new not nor none new nineteen name not new november nailed not not now nettles Nant-yr-Eira now new not not nature's never nurse nourished new name noisy nature night need notice neighbours[26] now notice narrator natural nag nothing notice nothing nothing name not nothing no[27] narrator nearest neighbour no night Nant Carfan[28] not new names nobody no narrator no nature neutral never negation need near nowhere not naked no night nothing never now no nobel[29] nature's new not nylons not nature nails (red) no not neighbour's new not ni not now next not news nothing nothing not now naming

O

out of on of out of of of of of old or over ordinary of of of orchard of of owls older on oak on old or old of of of of one or of on of of or of of on or on of on order of one or over of

P

Pail puckered parents plough pass provocative play ploughs pain porch praises poem praising polite priest peasant peat poetry praise Prytherch people print pane plough people play poems[30] picture pinned passed picture prospecting pastures preferring perhaps painting piety pattern peace past patient Prytherch piece passes proudly pasture pig phlegm proud pierced prating pluck power peasant peasant prompting perished people proud people people present present past people preferring people pulse pails ploughpastor peer pastors pastor peculiar Pugh Parry pulling properity playing Prytherch people parable place pavements past

Primary Texts

Data for the purchaser[31]

Possible

Chac Rain God of the Maya
Namandi malignant & lonely
Cynic follower of the eccentric Greek Philosopher
Diogenes
Mimir fount of wisdom
Ramanuja opposed to oneness
Ptah bearded
Zaddick lost in the mystic
Tawhirimatea fond of wind
Bodhidharma[32] sharp
Buddhagosa the commentator
Nyame the shining one
Obo pile of rocks

More Likely

the broken tractor
heat on high ground
bird
deer
hare
cattle
damp
the drained god
the land of rough grass
stack of bks bound in string

Q

Quiet

R

river racks rarer remember rising rook's resounded rain reluctant river refinments rhyme rill roof rule rain returned rich rare rooks rotting rain rattle rarely rich rarely riddle romantic ray rich recuperating roofs ripped Rhiannon rough Rhedynfre rain rain road ravages rattles roots Rhiannon's retreat red rivers relics right rain rattle rim red religion room remember rough righteous rim ruined round residue[33] rarely rain risk ripening rescued red random rubbing reborn R. rooting rnld[34] ring remote rain rain rooting roof reason remoter root removes roses return rigid roof road rivers rudeness[35] rhyme resinous reproves royal remote renewed rested raw restart[36] round

S

shoulders sharpness sweetness summer's shadow scaly sloughs soul sullied slurred stayed skin snow's sweet slow scene silence stars shy stairs stars sheep satisfaction sky shock stock stars study surface sapless shed silence sky shaggy-throated stars swords spears suckled sinew sky's suddenly sunder surrender sorrow stumbling spirit standpoint stinking same small star sunlight sheep something sheep sweaty shaken school strength source speech single speech skill sources[37] spring stone scathless scrawled school stranger saints shamed spilled spotted[38] scrawled shadow sheep seen sepulchre sealed settled spent sat scurrying stay sometimes sting sheep sty stable set squalls sharp

The Swedish Prize

Physics. Physiology. Literature.[39] Peace. Chemistry. Smokeless Powder.[40]

So

So language gets up

T

Tomos Twm Tomos turf tempered Tomos till tale Twm Twm Tomos's the the the tree to to till the the the thunder-browed thoated (shaggy) the there the the then the the that thronged the thundercloud tree this than the tree that the teach this the this the that the that than taken the thigh tendril the travelling the the the tie the to the to the the the the tongue the to that the the true the the that the that the tomb the the the the Twm[41] the therefore the turning[42] the the too to the too the the the the thatched the the too Ty'n-y-Fawnog there's the the the the the the that the the the the tongue the the the theirs the then though table the the the toad

Ned Thomas

It see mslik elyth atR.S.T omosfo undapers onalreso lution to this dilema by livingly incrept th rough the rough the rough the lip the land the rough language. There is heart clutching on Llyn. Join Ningtheland wagestu gglein recent years heha sbe combea def enderer the right. Right. To of about. Specifically of the Welsh. Once in a sidestrip runnig. His hair philosophic bent oft. But these are predictable. Decay. Expression. Distance.[43] Colonial structure. In the rhotoric of nationalism the Welsh wd spoke th air lang with pride, past, pride[44] expected, powerful, felt, fashion parallel like strut. Negat ively col onialstruc cool. End of backward glance. End of obscure assertion. End of laments. End of profoundest something to love, missed. End of discrediting. Negation, again, negative, unnecessary. Drive, driven and that. Focus and blur. Stuff imperialist criticism. In front of the fire / With you, the folk song / Of the wind in the chimney. Ned Thomaso[45].

U

under under unborn[46] uncurling uncouthness unnatural unconscious 'un under untidy unhappy under under unlearn unseen united ugly unleavened under under unchristened undone uncertainty under under undo understand under useless under undone under

V

veins vast verse vague valediction village veins vision
valleys vanished voice vestry valleys voice vein vast
village voices vain void vowels vixen vast vain view
variations verses verse

W

Welsh[47] whiteness wanting wrong[48] wind world welcome we wind's we who winds wades white wings with Welsh witted (half) wind's winner womb where world will where wantons whore whisperers wife wild winds woods with wind wind woods wide why when wind who who world white Wales wrenched wood whipped whose water wind whom wing whipped where well wild work wrote woman woman was with well warbler words with window what with winds wound weather Welsh with when were wild workshop[49] when what with world woke Wales window would with was wife watching which wind walls winter weak with wood wind willingly wide with women when was waving with were wait weaving with Welsh

X

experiments exchange expatriates

(later)
xtremities xagerated xploiter xample xcellent[50]

Y

yeilds youth yet yet youthful you Yeats[51] your your you your your you you youth young yr young yellow yellow yoked yard you year yet you yourself year's yours you young yours you youth young you'll you[52] you yet you your year's young years[53] your you you you you yet yes

Z

Zero

Notes

[1] About: With so many words why make more? These resources exist and need to be proclaimed. There is a thin line between data and information and another one between information and art. I am in the business of crossing these lines. Do we read our texts or do we store them on shelves? They lean into each other and meld. The memory puts in the connecting wires. And the machine stalled at an abyss, empty as the tomb in Palestine. The eternal afterdraught of the bone's dream.

[2] *see* endnote 1 above.

[3] *see* Finch, Peter, *Antibodies*, Stride 1997. Poem could be about the village off the A470 in north wales but is more likely to be a love affair.

[4] Dear Mr Finch, I wonder if you might be willing and able to help me in my search for a short poem by R.S. Thomas that was read on the Radio 4 programme, *Today*, in the Autumn of last year. I have searched several volumes of Thomas's poetry but to no avail. Ditto after hours on the internet. I have thoroughly enjoyed broadening my exposure to his work but remain frustrated at my failure. I cannot remember any of the lines except that I believe it is about his wife, Mildred Eldridge, and alludes to her being a solid presence when alive — his anchor — and how that solidity faded away after her death. I seem to recall the allusion being to do with either snow or sand. I would be hugely grateful if you can suggest which of R.S.'s poems this might be? Yours sincerely, Nick Salmon.

[5] *Wins:* R. S. Thomas has been presented the Cymrodorion Medal at his home at Pentrefelin, near Criccith. Half a century of writing. R.S.Thomas was the 50th person to receive the accolade in the 250-year history of the London-based Honourable Society of the Cymrodorion. Beth yw Cymrod rid rn? Now 87. "His work is read and appreciated worldwide and he has put Wales on the literary map by being the most prominent English-language poet of his day." Kyffin Williams was there. Pres Prof Emrys Jones. Wednesday 5th July, 2000. Same day the young poets launched *Oxygen*. R.S. was always fond of his.

[6] *see* Fans

[7] *see* X

[8] R.S.Thomas Information is a composition by Peter finch that explores the line between data and creativity. The piece contains deconstructed text, found material, collage and original work, along with actual information relating to Wales' greatest poet, R.S.Thomas. In keeping with the medium in which it is presented R.S.Thomas Information was assembled entirely on screen using the net itself as a resource. The hyper-text links speed assimilation, something the bard himself would probably hate. You can check this original at www.peterfinch.co.uk/depot.htm Comments on the composition are most welcome and are often incorporated into the ever evolving text. Write to the author c/o the publisher.

[9] *see* R

[10] *see* 8 above

[11] The Light. R S is striding down the hill through the early morning light. Clear, tight. His jaw stretches like paper. He hasn't shaved perfectly, bristles on the chin are missed. The fields behind him are full of mangles, green top, the soil in overgrown furrows. The hedges stand exactly where they did on the ancient maps. This landscape, his landscape, it doesn't change much.

In his hand he clutches a copy of Peter Meuiller's *Distaff* and the catalogue of book-bound objects showing at the European Centre for Traditional and Regional Culture at Llangollen, Clwyd. Childe Roland's paper book in a bottle, his bindings of torn paper, colours overlaid and rolling like waves, treaties with subject but no content, gestalt whiteness, French and welsh merging, fel melin, fel ymbarel, fel eli, fel melfa, fel tawel, fel dychwel, What are your plans for the future, my lord, Ham and Jam? There is light in these works; sometimes nothing but. Where else in this northern fastness can you find the word for light repeated so often that it glows. The friction of the signifier, the concrete base of Meuiller's brightness makes sparks in the Welsh air.

> *Childe Roland to the Dark Tower Came*. A poem by Robert Browning published in *Men and Women* (1855). The title comes from a snatch of song recited by Edgar in King Lear. To maintain his practice and his position Browning had resolved to write a poem a day. The Lear song comes from the age of Arthur where Childe Rowland, aided by the instruction of Merlin, makes his way to a castle to rescue his sister who has been carried there by fairies. "Child Rowland to the dark tower came, / His word was still 'Fie, foh, and fum / I smell the blood of a British man.'

R S hums the snatch, feet in their brogues crushing the earth clod, small dust flurries rise as they pass. The light here has never been good. No depth or range of colour, only grey and green. And the wind blowing. Meuiller in his guise as Childe Roland has adopted these lands. On them he mixes his native Canadian French with the Welsh of the stones. His dissertation was a blank book with a long line running from page one to page three hundred. The line was English, if a line can carry tongue. It sped from where the idea began to where the idea finished. Do ideas finish? R S is unsure.

On the headland facing Ynys Enlli, island of the saints, Bardsey, birds and graves, and holy stones, Roland has assembled a choir. Slowly they sing the Shearwater Oratorio – dit dit dah dit – Roland's Morse code translation of the Manx Shearwater's enigmatic cry. R S wasn't there. The text in his hands is colourless and silent. But on Bardsey, the shearwater's breeding ground, is a cloud of wings, a storm of sound.

R S walks on. You can't rely on things. He knows that. Childe Roland doesn't engage language from the outside. He assembles it from within. R S stuffs the poems inside his coat. Read them again later. Worry about the consequences. Or keep the whole thing a life secret? Behind him the sun's light streams in through the clouds. The paleness banished. Fel cerdd newydd. Nawr.

[12] *see* W

[13] *see* Primary Texts

[14] Finch, Peter, Glow (uncollected)

Clouds harvest stone moorland
Memory bones bracken fluttering
Baubles cowries rulers sunlight
God furrows worship tremble
Nothing fountain bitter flowers
Obstinacy gorging counsellors running
Weakness stubborn dark artificer

Nucleus religion charmer bacteria
Drowned suppurate fractured water
Idiot orchestra idiot laughter
Mangle departure death dreamer
Chaucer Pope Wales England
God hills quilts gardens
Hair men art comfort
Rig window rain-hammered dazzle

Gold conviction land light
Language music haunted stillness
Dance dust rafter flower
Gorse gyre halo breaking
Leaves sleep singing endless

[15] *see* Fans

[16] *see* Vee

[17] Finch, Peter, Hills — taken from *Poems For Ghosts (Seren* 1991).

> Just an ordinary man of the bald Welsh hills,
> docking sheep, penning a gap of cloud.
> Just a bald man of the ordinary hills,
> Welsh sheep gaps, docking pens, cloud shrouds.
> Just a man, ordinary, Welsh doctor, pen weaver
> cloud gap, sheep sailor, hills.
> Just a sharp shard, hill weaver, bald sheep,
> pilot pen rider, gap doctor, cloud.
> Just a shop, sheer hill weaver, slate,
> balder, cock gap, pen and Welsh rider,

Just slate shop, hill balder, cocking,
shop gap. Welsh man, cloud pen.
Just shops, slate, cocks, bald sheep,
Welsh idea, gutteral hills, ordinary cloud.
Just grass gap, bald gap, garp grap,
grap shot sheep slate, gap grap.

garp gap
gop gap
sharp grap shop shap
sheep sugar sha
shower shope sheep
shear shoe slap sap
grasp gap gosp gap
grip gap grasp gap
guest gap grat gap
gwint gap grog gap
growd gap gost gap
gap gap gwin gap
gap gop gwell gap
gap gop gap gap
gap gap gap gap
gap gap gorp gap
gap gap gap gap
gap gap gap gap
gap gap gap gap
gap gap gap gap
gap gap gap

immigrant slate mirth grot gap
bald grass, rock gap, rumble easy,
old gold gap, non-essential waste gap,
rock docker, slow slate gap, empty rocker,
rate payer, wast gap, cloud hater,
grasper balder, pay my money, dead,
trout shout, slate waste, language nobody
uses, bald sounds, sends, no one pens,
fire gap, failed gasps,
dock waste, holiday grey gap,
hounds, homes, plus fours, grip sheep,
four-wheeled Rover: Why not? Soft price,
grown gravel, sais

The problem gaps, ordinary television,
nationalist garbage, insulting ignorance,
shot sheep, invited bald interference,
don't need real sheep where we are,

sheepless, sheepless, Welsh as you are, still,
no gasps, gogs or gaps for us,
no,
point our aerials at the Mendip Hills.

Sat in the front row at the Jesus College, Oxford conference on bilingualism and translation was R.S.Thomas. On the platform Finch wondering if he should read *Hills*, a poem about language and Welsh television with its lifted and permutated first line. Should he acknowledge the Thomas source? Explain the poem? Read something else? He ploughs on. "This is poem which takes a famous line as its starting point," he says. His delivery is wound-up power. R.S.Thomas with his wild hair sits like a statue. His face does not flicker.

[18] *see* Composition Theory

[19] It is natural for human beings to be happy with works of imitation or representation. Rough and tumble happiness. Happiness overtook me when I was out of doors. I lost myself in an instant of perfect happiness. I was saturated with happiness sitting before you in the streaming sun. Four-levels of happiness. Trained happiness. Systems of happiness including luck. Unfair muscular happiness. Rejected animal magnetic happiness. Tamed and trained happiness. The happy subliminal virus is a possibility here. Pragmatic happy Iago thought about it in his surly landscape. This language is unhappy I shall refrain from speaking it. I shall sit wearing my sunday suit in this byre in the shade and floating motes with the soft sweat at the back of my collar until the time for the service comes round and instead of rising and preparing myself for faith and praise I shall stay on here in a somnambulant buzz. I shall not speak. I shall not go. Medical divining rods. The absent laughter of water. A great thinness covers us all.

Happiness hysteria. Happiness due a high workload is likely to be manipulation. There are also basic questions about happiness. Monk, T.H. and Folkard, S. (1985) Shiftwork and Happiness, Temporal Factors. Walker, J. (1982) Social Problems of Happiness, A British Perspective. Beaches as happiness. The long rocks and the soft sand. The happy dog. The sandcastle. Casual happiness follows correlation. Environmental happiness and the stress buster. All these gargoyles smiling at me all the time.

Linguistic happiness. Y rwyf' rhywbeth hapus iawn. Hapus nawr. The pragmatic happiness after done book, that moment when the poem is just complete and the world is bright before the doubt starts, before the need to repeat arrives, before the can I, before the will I, before the is it, before the does it, before the itch and gnawing, before that. The smile of happiness. State of happiness: required as shoring against ruin. The sea comes in here faster than anywhere else in Western Europe. You can see the glints on the wave tops as the detergent foam flecks the air. There is a sky full of birds. Their thin hearts are happy. Their minds are like water-beds. Their happiness is a blessing. It can never be a curse.

Happiness as the pre-supposition of original sin. The hapiness in sin, or happiness as the consequence of sin in the particular individual. Happiness as a saving experience by means of faith. Happiness and faith are not the same.

Causes:

breath
ozone (look up)
left the past
the great painting
bardo distrust
bone marrow removed replaced with hand cream
work accepted by *Parataxis*

I am so happy now. Hop hoop. Harp. Hu har. hip hip. huh. H'm.Blood clear. Apt and opportune. Bones comfortable. No clatter (*see endnote 3 above*). Elegant skin. A pullover. Such fun.

[20] *see* Y

[21] *see* S

[22] *see* Fans

[23] *see* The Light, 11 above

[24] Laureate Nobel. Dynamite maker. Prizes awarded by the Swedish Academy for literature. The prize which is worth about £35,000 depending on capital is awarded from the income of a capital sum. The sum of the economics. The sum is an annual dependant on accumulation. The little sum sits and the little sum sits and the little sum sits and the sum gets up bigger. The sum is vital.

The parts leak like running dogs. So many little sums. All the little sums in the world. No distinction for nationality nor sex. No little sum gets into bed. The prize lingers like a falling star on the back of the retina. The names clatter (*see note 3 above)* like falling rain. Fashions twists the sum like the sum like income like the pull of beards replaced by shaved cheeks.

The accumulation shores against. The way when you get you don't know the way that did was did could have but came anyway sum in its pocket and the rolling forward is the thing you never knew but it's here anyway. The future. The sum. The many sums. The accumulation. The collected. The special edition. The way it is like a fist of. Economics elder brother to falling. This time it's rising. Sum of the sums. Great power. No truce anywhere. Didn't win.

[25] *see* F

[26] *see* X

[27] Would he have accepted a commission to write a poem for the Millennium? Not a chance

[28] *see* Jubblepoint

[29] *see* 24 above

[30] *see* Page X [insert here contents page of this book]

[31] Titles in print from the following list can be obtained through Amazon and/or Gwales:

Song At the Year's Turning 1942-54 — *Rupert Hart-Davies, 1955*

Poetry For Supper — *Rupert Hart-Davies, 1958*

Tares — *Rupert Hart-Davies, 1961*

The Bread Of Truth — *Rupert Hart-Davies, 1963*

Pieta — *Rupert Hart-Davies, 1966*

Not That He Brought Flowers — *Rupert Hart-Davies, 1968*

Young And Old — *Chatto & Windus, 1972*

H'm — *Macmillan, 1972*

Selected Poems, 1946-1968 — *MacGibbon/Hart-Davies, 1973*

What Is A Welshman? -*Christopher Davies, 1974*

Laboratories Of The Spirit — *Macmillan, 1975*

The Way Of It — *Ceolfrith Press, 1977*

Frequencies — *Macmillan, 1975*

Between Here And Now — *Macmillan, 1981*

Later Poems 1972-1982 — *Macmillan, 1983*

Ingrowing Thoughts — *Poetry Wales Press, 1985*

Destinations — *Celandine Press, 1985*

Neb — *Gwasg Gwynedd, 1985*

Experimenting With An Amen — *Macmillan, 1986*

Selected Poems, 1946-1968 -*Bloodaxe Books, 1986*

Welsh Airs — *Poetry Wales Press, 1987*

The Echoes Return Slow — *Macmillan, 1988*

Blwyddyn Yn Llyn — *1990*

Counterpoint — *Bloodaxe Books, 1990*

Pe Medrwn Yr Iaith — *1990*

Cymru Or Wales — *Gwasg Gomer, 1992*

Mass For Hard Times — *Bloodaxe Books, 1992*

Collected Poems 1945-1990 — *Dent, 1993*

No Truce With The Furies — *Bloodaxe Books, 1995*

Selected Prose — *1995*

Selected Poems — *1996*

Autobiographies — *1997*

R S Thomas Reading Poems — *Sain triple CD, 1999*

Collected Poems *1945-1990* — *2001*

Residues — *Bloodaxe Books, 2002*

Selected Poems — *Penguin, 2004*

Collected Later Poems 1988-2000 — *Bloodaxe, 2004*

[32] *see* Affinity

[33] Happy collapse smile astigmatism embroidering happier voice cold failed dove timelessness apologise insanity meaning cosmetic fauna sharpness crepuscular hotter pedestals golden vertigo anaesthetic syphilitic shrivelling radioactive rainbow spectrum ashen ammunition purse forestalled messenger alas foundations renaissance machine camera anonymity arid aircraft god unscalable depopulated graduates breath shanks perfume panting God body dance dismissed camel bone pearl machinery ersatz gold faith kiss bones moustache bosoms mirror music God flesh insect grey haemorrhage anchor soul sour sang God stripling stop science skulls shining soul spirit sea skulls stand Schubert she summon strokes stone speed stones space-time sing saying scholarly swivels shapeless self sorry shinning spirit something something song stipulated periscopes grass repose prose stones syntax god soar spirits fresh tired odes

Residues, the final poems of R S Thomas, published posthumously on 25th July, 2002 by Bloodaxe Books. In these late poems Thomas wrestles with the silence of God

[34] Finch, Peter, RNLD TOMOS (Originally published in *Food – Seren, 1997)* but this revised version from Robin Reeves' *New Welsh Review, 2000)*

> (vcl, hca, some prse) aka Curtis Langdon. 1913-2000. Gospel. Austerity tradition. Jnd Iago Prytherch Big Band (1959), notch, crack, gog, gap, bwlch, tan, iaith, mynydd, mangle, adwy — mainly on Hart-Davis race label. Reissue Dent PoBkSoc Speial Recommnd. Concert at Sherman support Sorley Maclean (gtr, hrt clutching) sold out. Fire Bomb tour Sain triple cd for D Walford Davies (vcl, crtcl harmonium) new century highspot. A pioneer of dark wounds and internal tensions. In old age bird song and reliable grouch. Stood, was counted, still no change. To live in Wales is to become unassailable. "An Angel Fish" (Clarke). Expect retrospective, marvelling and statue.

[35] *see* M

[36] *see* AAAAA

[37] Sources:
R.S.Thomas: *No Truce With The Furies*, Bloodaxe Books 1995
R.S.Thomas: *Collected Poems 1945 — 1990*, Dent 1993
R S Thomas: *Residues*, Bloodaxe Books 2002
M. Wynn Thomas (editor): *The Page's Drift — R.S.Thomas at Eighty*, Seren 1993
Elaine Shepherd: *R.S.Thomas: Conceding An Absence* — Macmillan Press, 1995
Meic Stephens (editor): *The Oxford Companion To The Literature Of Wales*, OUP 1986

[38] Peter, Did you know that RS has recently moved to Criccieth? Previously he was living in a small cottage adjacent to the Plas Brondanw estate (the Clough Williams Ellis place). We saw him standing outside there last Summer. He was recently seen walking down the middle of the road in Porthmadog — too many people on the pavements! All the best, Gill

[39] *see* 24 above

[40] *see* EEEEEEE EEEEE EEE E EEEE

[41] a fan

[42] *see* Composition Theory

[43] *see* I

[44] *see* Possible

[45] *see* Italian language edition (forthcoming)

[46] *see* ZEE

[47] *see* D

[48] Dear Colleague, The forward written by Andrew Motion in the Phoenix Press reprinting of R.S. Thomas *Collected Poems 1945-1990* states that: 'he (R.S.Thomas) was a Church of England priest who ministered in Wales to a largely Non-Conformist (sic) congregation'; this of course is blatantly incorrect. R.S. Thomas was a minister of Church in Wales from 1936 and his congregation was Anglican. This ministry was crucial to his life and work. Because Andrew Motion and Phoenix Press have carelessly published this false information it will be perceived as the truth unless it is rescinded, consequently the life and work of R.S. Thomas will misrepresented and misunderstood. Please would you e-mail Andrew Motion and Bing Taylor, Managing Director of Phoenix Press at (rbt@orionbooks.co.uk) to 'request' that this forward is rescinded, corrected and republished, please could you also publicise this mistake in whatever way available to you. With best wishes, Christine (Kinsey), July 12th, 2002.

[51] *see* Fans

[52] *see* mmm

[53] *see* Pee

Notes on *The Welsh Poems*

The Welsh Poems brings together poems and other texts made since Stride published *Antibodies* and Seren published *Food* in 1997. They are largely left-field, innovative pieces that operate at the far edges of what poetry is understood to be. They are the *Welsh* poems in tribute to John James whose own book of the same title, published in 1967, was an early influence and because that's what they are: Welsh. They are texts which sometimes have as their subject the matter of Wales. As examples of the politically incorrect they occasionally move between two languages, melding and manipulating. Macaronic works. Poems with no certain home.

Aficionados of technique will find the found, the extracted, the bent and processed, the recycled, the cut and pasted, the masqued, the flailed, the rubbed, the ripped and the repeated here. They will encounter Oulipo. They will discover dada. They will enjoy daub, drip and smear. They'll also find the new, plucked straight from the air.

Poems are poems because the poet says they are. These are Welsh Poems. My nomenclature.

The notes which follow are not exhaustive and in some cases may appear to explain little. Work has to be left for the reader. Often it is just that tension which makes the poem work.

Fold — (cant)(explain)(can) (might) (read on)

Colon — these are all Welsh battles, battles on Welsh soil. Data on the early battles is scant and often just who was fighting and with whom their were allied is difficult to discern. Strange alliances existed and a lot of blood was lost. An army was more than 36 men. Less than that then the fighting unit was known as a war band. These listed were big battles, great clashes, and always they were ones in which the Welsh lost.

Historians — From a review by Felipe Fernandez-Armestro in *The Times* 6/2/1997.

Rev (again) — The winter 1997 issue of the journal *Poetry Wales* carried a review of my collection *Useful* written by Ian Macmillan. It ended with the challenge: "What he should do now is rework this review into a poem." The piece originally appeared as a component of *The Peter Finch Archive*. Ian Macmillan may never have seen it. He will now.

Cover Blown — William Burroughs, arch-Beat and world-class literary experimenter reputedly wore little other than grey suits in order to remain permanently anonymous.

Pantycelyn: The Tools & Things Version — after the poem on the Rev. William Williams, Pantycelyn, one of the major figures of the Welsh Methodist Revival of the 18th century by D Gwenallt Jones (1899-1969).

newjobs — the dolig sodder first appeared in *Some Christmas Haiku* in *Food* (Seren 1997).

Wobble — written using techniques borrowed from La Bibliothèque Oulipienne, the library of the literary movement *Oulipo* — Ouvroir de Littérature Potentielle, or Workshop of Potential Literature, a group of writers and mathematicians. Members include Raymond Queneau, François Le Lionnais, Claude Berge, Georges Perec, and Italo Calvino. The group was founded in Paris in 1960

Rhai Caneuon Cymraeg — Some Welsh songs.

Mid Period Anglo-Welsh Endings – in my early encounters with what was then known as Anglo-Welsh Writing (which has since been re-classified as the slick and readily marketable 'Welsh Writing In English') works were distinguished by the number of Welsh place names and/or Welsh loan words they contained.

Slide Guitar Devices — the room is dark, tobacco smoke, low watt light bulbs, shades brown with nicotine. Someone up front with a guitar on their knee. Strap hung with horse brasses. Coloured tags. Capo. Lapel badges. Foot on box. Tapping. Open tuning, unstrung, twisted, hums. Used: lipstick holder, steel comb, aluminium cigar case, bottle neck, drinking glass, junior hack-saw, biro, costume ring, umbrella middle, piece of ice. Watching like hawks. Plug in the amp blue roar and splintering. Ear warp. Floor. Floor. Applause.

Tick In Box — Williams, Williams, Williams, Henri, Williams, Finch.

Pitt Rivers — the Oxford archaeological and ethnographic museum.

How To Speak (1) and *How To Speak (2)* – dynamic versions of these poems can be viewed at the Peter Finch Archive – www.peterfinch.co.uk

Slow To Change — commissioned by Rupert Loydell for Stride's new online magazine. Rupert wanted pieces that showed how we were and how we are and how the movement between the two is never as fast as we think.

Easy X-rays — synizesis socioeconomic abhorred pasturage octa- marginal unstring complacent hammer and sickle deceleration solvents established hepper Addis augur sophists point out long-snouted Glinka cologne infections. nonmoral lovespoon burmeisteri serenely Northallerton de-icer mushroom-like Alcidae tbs. hyperaemia scoop sonneteer outskirts Midnight Anu ear deplorable Gruy poind A.D conservatory greenstick Berwick-upon-Tweed flaunch dariole Jehoshaphat stationary bills Llandudno Llysfaen Rhyl Colwyn Bay Prestatyn Book of Welsh Tea-Shop Walks Sickness Marduk magnitudes basen Nycticebus roulette transposition plaques unloaded dotty biparous eyelash brightness valgus rockoon Bruchidae three-legged farinose piece Bemba seconde rank. pardoner Vibrio Philosophia hammering Newham feaze improper integral Hsinking dulcis heptameter mangles vestrymen mangabey fricandeau printer objectivity betulus drifts

Llywarch Hen SMS with fault – a translation from the ninth century Welsh poem.

Before 1962 — Rock and roll guitar instrumentals Roy Orbison Craig Douglas Bobby Rydell Lonnie Donnegan Tommy Steele Billy Cotton early Phil Spector

Uncle Mac no beat music every little breath I take falsetto lots of dances much touching. Boogie woogie if you were liberal. Quickstep and waltz if you were not.

Damage — a tribute piece for the late Bob Cobbing, written the mark his life.

Cardiff Medicine — As you age your contact with the health system increases. Knowing where the hospital is becomes an obsession. History leaks through it. Hobson Matthew's great six volume transcription of the records of Cardiff was published at the end of the nineteenth century and the start of the twentieth in an edition of only four hundred. My set is number 32 and once graced the shelves of the library of Howells Girls School. These texts — with some personal interference and a few typical Finch asides — form the basis for this poem.

Brudge — sonnet written for William Wordsworth's *Composed on Westminster Bridge* celebrations in 2002.

Recycle — after William Carlos Williams.

Bg Hrt — visual sonnet written for William Wordsworth's *Composed on Westminster Bridge* celebrations in 2002. Not performed from the stage at the Globe, although the offer was there.

Literature — lines taken from a range of early twentieth century Anglo-Welsh novels.

Residues — R S Thomas' posthumous collection published by Bloodaxe in 2002 and edited by M Wynn Thomas.

Past Interests — a reworking of the answer to a question on influences put to me by Andy Brown for his book *Binary Myths*. The making of lists has been a twentieth century obsession. In these Welsh Poems it is finally expunged.

Ysbwriel — an early version of the text which now runs along the top of the Lamby Way landfill site at the mouth of the River Rumney in Cardiff. This was written as a result of an Arts & Regeneration Agency CBAT commission to work with the Dutch artists Jeroen van Westen.

> "I work the words. In Welsh, faint langauge of these soggy lands centuries back, it's ysbwriel, frewcsach, rwbish, fflwcs. The way the Welsh language has so much wealth fascinates me. What the hell are fflwcs? How did they arrive? Jeroen gets the versions by e-mail, makes his suggestions, then tosses them back. He wants the deal in capitals with dots at x height. There's an echo of a Celtic / Roman / David Jones back-glance here but so slight you wouldn't notice.
>
> WASTE•CYCLE•GLE•SBWRIEL•FFLWCS•BGS•BLK•WAS•A•IS•A•BACK •AS•A•NEW•IS•NWY•GAS
>
> Does that look like Tolkien? Like Eric Gill? It does not. How does it sound? What are these words like when they talk in the air? I find an old computer headset and read a version into my pc, get carried away by

the rhythm and double its length. E-mail it to Holland. Finch spwriel-speak in the ether. Out there.

I need to pursue the fflwcs connection. What is this word? Who recognises it. Older, south east-Wales Welsh, the dictionary tells me. I ask around. Results are inconclusive. I bump into Dafydd El at an Earthfall reception at Chapter. What does he think? He offers to check. I e-mail it in. He bangs it round the Cynulliad and I get a fulsome multi-layered response by return. Fflwcs is recognised as meaning rubbish by enough respondents. It's a word from the south, one that would have had a currency here when Cardiff was a walled-town and the Rumney was clean and clear. Fflwcs is overgrowth, weed. The stuff a farmer would scrape as useless from his field's surface and leave to rot, to heat, to turn to gas. Weed-flowers. Phlox. The piece turns, flies between Cardiff and the Netherlands, switches, gets half-rhyme, gets discussed, gets longer, gets cut.

WASTE•CYCLE•RECYCLE•GLE••SBWRIEL••GRASS•GASH•FFLW
CS•BGS•NEW•BLK•BAGS••ISA•WSA•BACK••IS•A•NWY•NEW••S•
A••NEWGAS"

— taken from *Real Cardiff Two* (Seren, 2004).

Cheng Man Ch'ing — Yang-style tai chi master

Tea Room — my companion was Bob Cobbing

Torrance — Chris Torrance, open field poet master, Beacon's hermit, lover of ley lines and creator of wonderful texts.

www.ingramcontent.com/pod-product-compliance
Lightning Source LLC
Chambersburg PA
CBHW032051150426
43194CB00006B/497
9780907562917